MW00905720

GOD'S
MEGATHEMES
A GRANDFATHER'S LEGACY

JIM PHILLIPS

Jim Phillips

WESTBOW
PRESS®
A DIVISION OF THOMAS NELSON
& ZONDERVAN

Scriptures taken from the Holy Bible, New International Version®, NIV®. Copyright © 1973, 1978, 1984, 2011 by Biblica, Inc.™ Used by permission of Zondervan. All rights reserved worldwide. www.zondervan.com The "NIV" and "New International Version" are trademarks registered in the United States Patent and Trademark Office by Biblica, Inc.™

This book is a work of non-fiction. Unless otherwise noted, the author and the publisher make no explicit guarantees as to the accuracy of the information contained in this book and in some cases, names of people and places have been altered to protect their privacy.

WestBow Press books may be ordered through booksellers or by contacting:

WestBow Press
A Division of Thomas Nelson & Zondervan
1663 Liberty Drive
Bloomington, IN 47403
www.westbowpress.com
1 (866) 928-1240

Because of the dynamic nature of the Internet, any web addresses or links contained in this book may have changed since publication and may no longer be valid. The views expressed in this work are solely those of the author and do not necessarily reflect the views of the publisher, and the publisher hereby disclaims any responsibility for them.

Any people depicted in stock imagery provided by Getty Images are models, and such images are being used for illustrative purposes only. Certain stock imagery © Getty Images.

ISBN: 978-1-9736-2077-8 (sc)
ISBN: 978-1-9736-2079-2 (hc)
ISBN: 978-1-9736-2078-5 (e)

Library of Congress Control Number: 2018902257

Print information available on the last page.

WestBow Press rev. date: 03/06/2018

ACKNOWLEDGMENTS

This Grandfather's Legacy represents a lifetime collection of truths from scripture I want to share with family, friends, and any who desire to be a better follower of Jesus. This work wouldn't be in your hands without the support of many people, beginning with Ann, my wife of over forty years. Her devoted partnership in our service to Jesus and her constant encouragement to write have been a gift from God (James 1:17). I am also grateful for the numerous churches, pastors, and organizations, such as the C. S. Lewis Institute, who have afforded me the opportunity to learn and teach.

I want to thank several people who directly contributed to this work. I have been blessed with wonderful mentors and teachers, especially during my tenure with the C. S. Lewis Institute. I am grateful for these men: Dr. Ken Boa, Dr. Randy Newman, Dr. Art Lindsley, Dr. Joel Woodruff, Dr. Tom Tarrants, Tom Simmons, Jim Hiskey, Sigval Berg, John Bishop, Rear Admiral Alan (Blues) Baker, and George Anderson. I am also grateful to Brian Koger, whose gift for editing made these thoughts readable.

INTRODUCTION

Mine is not a story of dramatic conversion but of Jesus's faithfulness through good and bad times. I don't remember a time when I didn't love Jesus. I surrendered my life to Him in a small church in Little Rock, Arkansas, when I was thirteen years old. I remember asking Him to "live my life through me and use my life for His purpose."

Mine is a story of grace-enabled service to Jesus despite my weaknesses and failures. He has always been the lover of my soul, even when I strayed from Him. He has healed my wounds, answered my prayers, guided my steps, hugged me when I was down, communed with me when I was lonely, walked with me through difficult circumstances, and limited the consequences of my failures.

I have never doubted His existence. He is as real to me as any person I meet and speak with during the day, only He is always with me.

My only regrets are the times I failed Him. Sometimes my repentance was immediate, and other times repentance followed long after the sin. Yet He shielded me from the full consequence of my sins and (as He did with Peter) restored me to Himself, for which I am grateful. Once after one of my biggest failures, as I was wondering whether He could ever love me again, if things could ever be the same between us, He reminded me that He'd loved me before my sin, knowing that I would sin. I then fell in love with Him more deeply than ever.

For many years I was envious of people who had dramatic testimonies of being rescued from darkness into the light. But after experiencing the regret that followed my sins, I'm grateful that He answered my boyhood prayer and has been faithful to live my life through me and keep me for His service. I believe this is His desire for everyone. Give yourself to Him and see what He will do.

My life scripture (the passage most encapsulating my walk with Jesus) is Psalm 71:17–18 (NIV).

> Since my youth, O God, you have taught me,
> and to this day I declare your marvelous deeds.
> Even when I am old and gray,
> do not forsake me, O God,
> till I declare your power to the next generation,
> your might to all who are to come.

It is the two verses of this passage that require me to write these accumulations of truths I have learned while walking with Jesus.

Having enjoyed a full life, with many intimate times with Jesus, I have often been told, "You should write about that." Each time I took this matter to Jesus and asked whether this was where I should spend my time, and each time He restrained me from doing so. Recently, however, while undergoing a transition from full-time service in an information technology firm to service in the C. S. Lewis Institute and the Graduate Institute at Saint John's College, I petitioned Jesus again about the opportunity to write.

Soon after this, a senior pastor (and longtime follower of Jesus) asked me to have lunch with him. After ordering our food, the pastor began to speak to me with "thoughts from his heart." It was at the end of our conversation that he said to me, "Oh, one other thing; it is time for you to write—leave a legacy!" I have received only encouragement and no further restraints from Jesus since that time.

I write this to pass on what I have learned about Jesus, His Father, and the Spirit (the triune God); and to express how grateful that my parents and their friends introduced me to Him very early.

Many years ago, I began collecting truths about God that I found occurred repeatedly in His word (scripture) and that I have found to be true in the experiences of everyday life (existential truth). I began to refer to this collection of truths as "God's megathemes" because they are lessons He wants us to understand, so He repeats them throughout His written word to us.

What follows is a lifetime collection of biblical truths—megathemes—God has given to us to help us experience the life He intends us to have. I share them with you in hopes that you will grow in intimacy with God and come to value Him above all other things and persons.

MEGATHEME: AN EXISTENTIAL TRUTH SCRIPTURE REPEATEDLY EXPRESSES

Each chapter in this book is part of a story God wants you to understand. That is, each chapter is its own megatheme, but within each chapter are several other megathemes that reinforce the chapter heading.

Since these are megathemes, one would expect many biblical references to support each truth, so they are offered immediately after each truth claim. I then offer commentary and occasionally personal experiences to support the biblical truth. A word of caution: Personal experience can be instructive when it is evaluated in the light of biblical truth, but one should never use personal experience to evaluate and interpret scripture. Scripture should be the lens by which all other experiences are evaluated, not the reverse.

Father, please use the words that follow to draw all who read them into a closer relationship with You. Give them the greatest blessing they can ever receive: intimacy with You. Amen.

CONTENTS

GOD AND HIS WORD ARE TRUSTWORTHY

If this chapter title weren't true, I would have taken a different path long ago and relied on the strength and wisdom of another god, or no god, instead of God. The following passages (and many others) say all God's ways are loving and steadfast, never wavering, and what He says—His word—will always achieve its purpose.

> Know therefore that the Lord your God is God; he is the faithful God, keeping his covenant of love to a thousand generations of those who love him and keep his commands. (Deut. 7:9 NIV)

> All the ways of the Lord are loving and faithful for those who keep the demands of his covenant.
> (Ps. 25:10 NIV)

> Because of the Lord's great love we are not consumed, for his compassions never fail.
> They are new every morning;
> great is your faithfulness.
> (Lam. 3:22–23 NIV)

> So is my word that goes out from my mouth:
> It will not return to me empty,

but will accomplish what I desire
and achieve the purpose for which I sent it.
(Isa. 55:11 NIV)

Before we begin any discussion of who God is and what He does, we must be sure we can trust His word to be true. This is our first megatheme.

MEGATHEME 1:

SCRIPTURE CAN BE TRUSTED

If this megatheme isn't true, then all other megathemes are in doubt. Scripture is either trustworthy and has authority in our lives and discussions, or it's just another book offering opinions about how we should live our lives.

I don't intend to do an exhaustive apologetic for why we can trust scripture. Many others have done this very effectively, and I offer Dr. Ken Boa's essay "How Accurate Is the Bible?" in the appendix. I do, however, want to share a narrative you can use when others ask why scripture can be trusted.

1. We know our New Testament (NT) is 99.5 percent accurate compared to the original manuscripts (see the appendix).
2. The NT was written in the lifetime of eyewitnesses to Jesus's birth, miracles, death, and resurrection.
3. Therefore, the NT can be trusted.
4. The NT affirms the divinity of Christ; it says Jesus was resurrected. Jesus claimed to be God and foretold His resurrection as a sign of His divinity. He was resurrected; therefore, He is the ultimate authority on matters of God, life, death, truth and so forth.
5. Therefore, Jesus's teachings can be trusted.
6. Jesus affirmed the Old Testament (OT) at least nine times with sayings such as. "These are the Scriptures that testify

about me" (John 5:39 NIV). He spoke of places and persons in the OT as real, not fictional. Here are just a few of the passages where Jesus affirmed the scriptures:

Jesus replied, "You are in error because you do not know the Scriptures or the power of God." (Matt. 22:29 NIV)

"Haven't you read," he replied, "that at the beginning the Creator 'made them male and female,' and said, 'For this reason a man will leave his father and mother and be united to his wife, and the two will become one flesh'? So they are no longer two, but one. Therefore what God has joined together, let man not separate." (Matt. 19:4–6 NIV)

"If he called them 'gods,' to whom the word of God came—and the Scripture cannot be broken." (John 10:35 NIV)

Sanctify them by the truth; your word is truth. (John 17:17 NIV)

And beginning with Moses and all the Prophets, he explained to them what was said in all the Scriptures concerning himself. (Luke 24:27 NIV)

You diligently study the Scriptures because you think that by them you possess eternal life. These are the Scriptures that testify about me, yet you refuse to come to me to have life. (John 5:39–40 NIV)

But what "Scriptures" was Jesus referring to? Josephus recorded that a complete copy of the Hebrew scriptures was preserved in the temple in AD 37. The Dead Sea Scrolls, discovered in 1947, had a set of manuscripts that had been placed in the caves in AD 68. Those documents dated from 300 BC to AD 40. There were fragments of every book in our modern canon except Esther. It confirmed the accuracy of our translations for the past thousand years and that the OT canon was in place in 200 BC. This is the set of scriptures Jesus affirmed.

7. Therefore, the OT can be trusted.

You might look at it this way: once you demonstrate the accuracy of the NT, which declares the divinity of Christ, you get the OT thrown in for free because Christ affirmed it.

There are some other interesting things to consider in determining the trustworthiness of scripture:

8. The Bible provides existential truth; it best explains life as we see and experience it. I don't know anyone who kept the Ten Commandments and regretted it; I know many who broke a commandment and had remorse for doing so.
9. The scriptures have archeological validation; there have been no archeological contradictions to the claims of scripture. In fact, the Bible is one of the most trusted handbooks for archaeologists.
10. The scriptures contain over twenty-five hundred prophecies. Two thousand have been fulfilled without error, and five hundred occur in the future.
11. The whole is greater than the sum of its parts—evidence of divine authorship. The story of Moriah and its significance as the place where God would satisfy His wrath for the sins of humankind spans the time from Abraham through Christ (two thousand years), and many authors give us a story none of them could foresee: Christ, the perfect Lamb, sacrificed for the sins of the world on the very site where Isaac was spared. This is the place where the angel of God sheathed his sword

after David made the sacrifice to appease God's wrath for taking the census of his people.

Now I want to offer an even simpler narrative. If God could create a Y chromosome in a virgin's womb to produce the God-man and perform so many miracles "the world would not have room for the books that could be written" (John 21:25), and if He could resurrect His Son after Christ suffered a horrible and disfiguring death, is He not able to preserve His word so we aren't misled by what we read today?

Of all the apologetics arguing for the reliability of scripture, I believe the strongest is its existential truth. C. S. Lewis said in "Is Theology Poetry?" "I believe in Christianity as I believe that the sun has risen: not only because I see it, but because by it I see everything else."

Scripture explains the world best as I see and experience it, and I find its precepts are true independent of popular or cultural opinion. If we can trust God's word to be true, does it reveal to us a God who can be trusted? This leads us to our second megatheme.

MEGATHEME 2:

WHEN GOD ACTS, THIS ALWAYS RESULTS IN THE GREATEST GOOD FOR THE GREATEST NUMBER AND FOR THE LONGEST PERIOD

Now that is a far-reaching statement. Where in scripture does it say that?

While those exact words aren't found in scripture, there are a number of passages that speak to the patience, kindness, and goodness of God.

> And the Lord said, "I will cause all my goodness to pass in front of you, and I will proclaim my name, the Lord, in your presence. I will have mercy on whom I

will have mercy, and I will have compassion on whom I will have compassion." (Ex. 33:19 NIV)

But you, O Lord, are a compassionate and gracious God, slow to anger, abounding in love and faithfulness. (Ps. 86:15 NIV)

Rend your heart
and not your garments.
Return to the Lord your God,
for he is gracious and compassionate,
slow to anger and abounding in love,
and he relents from sending calamity.
(Joel 2:13 NIV)

Or do you show contempt for the riches of his kindness, tolerance and patience, not realizing that God's kindness leads you toward repentance? (Rom. 2:4)

There is no shortage of such verses, but this megatheme is better validated by looking at biblical stories and recognizing that the entire Old Testament after the fall (Gen. 3) is about God providing for humankind's redemption. The Old Testament is all about Christ. Every story, event, and detail in some way relates to Christ and His coming into the world to reconcile the world and humans to God. That being said, it's safe to say that every act of God in the Old Testament, direct or indirect, results in the greatest good for the greatest number and for the longest period—the coming of our Lord and Savior, Jesus Christ. We can see this fact more clearly by looking at some of the stories in scripture.

CREATION OF THE UNIVERSE

Have you ever wondered why, of the infinite number of universes God could have created, He made this one, the one you and I live in? Unlike many other "gods," God didn't need His creation to self-actualize. Before there were angels or a universe with humans, there was the triune God—Father, Son, and Spirit. They were enjoying the fellowship of one another. That is, they were perfectly complete—without need—in their community of three. Yet God created a spiritual universe with spiritual beings; then He created a physical universe and populated it with living things, including humans. Why did God create at all, and why this universe?

The answer to the first question leads to the answer to the second. God created not just because He could but because He wanted to share what He could offer—eternal life—with "children" or offspring who would experience life: sunrises, spring showers, walks in the garden, snow-covered mountains, gentle sea breezes, and thunderstorms. I am eternally grateful that God decided to create the universe to include you and me, and I believe our gratitude was one of the reasons He did.

But why this world, one that, while having the characteristics above, is also fraught with pain and suffering? Because if God's reason for creating was to create beings who could glory in His creation, His gift of life, then it's reasonable that of all the possible worlds He could create, He would choose the world that would allow His creatures free will—the freedom to choose or reject His offer of eternal life—and result in the greatest possible number of people accepting His offer. That is, of all the possible worlds God could have created, He chose the one in which the most are saved, and the fewest are lost. And further, none are lost in this world who would have been saved in another.

To the first point, this is the world in which the most are saved and the fewest are lost.

> The Lord is not slow in keeping his promise, as some understand slowness. He is patient with you, not wanting anyone to perish, but everyone to come to repentance. (2 Peter 3:9 NIV)

> From one man he made every nation of men, that they should inhabit the whole earth; and he determined the times set for them and the exact places where they should live. God did this so that men would seek him and perhaps reach out for him and find him, though he is not far from each one of us. (Acts 17:26–27 NIV)

These verses suggest God not only wants all to be saved but also has determined the time and place where we would be born (which includes the universe He made) so we would have the best opportunity to find Him.

Here's the second point. No one will be lost in this world who would have been saved in another. We need to realize that none of us would exist in any other world. All the choices of free men and women (beginning with Adam and Eve when they conceived their first child, their second, and so forth) would be different, and you and I wouldn't be here.

How does the creation of the world validate our megatheme? This single act was the greatest good (that eternal existence could be offered to the nonexistent) for the greatest number (because God chose a world where the most will accept His offer and the fewest will reject Him) and for the longest period (the life God offers is eternal— an eternal, intimate relationship with Him).

SUFFERINGS OF JOB

The next two examples supporting the truth of this megatheme involve an indirect act of God and suffering on behalf of the central figure (Job). All things come through the hands of God, both good and evil. Some things He does directly (such as the creation of the universe), and others He allows (does indirectly) by working through the free choices of men and women, natural causes (earthquakes, volcanoes, hurricanes, tornadoes, and so forth), or even the actions of Satan and demons.

Job's story (Job 1–42) is a fascinating account of a man suffering after a conversation between God and Satan. It is generally agreed that Job is one of the oldest books of scripture and that he may have been a contemporary of Abraham, which would place the book of Job somewhere around or immediately after Genesis 12. God offered Job to Satan as an example of a righteous man. "Then the Lord said to Satan, 'Have you considered my servant Job? There is no one on earth like him; he is blameless and upright, a man who fears God and shuns evil'" (Job 1:8 NIV).

Satan challenged God and claimed Job's admiration and affection for Him was purely utilitarian—that is, Job worshipped and honored God because he received blessings from God. God knew Job's heart and allowed him to fall into Satan's hands for a time so through the fire of testing all would see that Job's affection for God was based on the intrinsic qualities of God—His worthiness to be worshipped—and not on Job's expectation of receiving things from God.

You know the story: the suffering Job endured, the lack of comfort he received from his well-meaning friends, the loss of family and health. So how can we say this was for good, much less the greatest good for the greatest number and for the longest period?

During Job's suffering, he asked three questions:

> But how can a mortal be righteous before God? (Job 9:2 NIV)

> If only there were someone to arbitrate between us,
> to lay his hand upon us both,
> someone to remove God's rod from me. (Job 9:33–34 NIV)

If a man dies, will he live again? (Job 14:14 NIV)

Those three profound questions are asked at the very beginning of the written word:

1. How can sinful man stand before a holy God?
2. Is there anyone who can intercede for us and remove God's wrath from us?
3. If we die, will we live again?

The rest of scripture sets out to answer Job's questions, and those answers are the following:

1. Through Jesus by accepting His finished work on the cross
2. Yes. Jesus, who sits at the right hand of the Father, intercedes for us.
3. Yes, we will live again through Jesus, whose resurrection not only validated His claim to deity but also assured our resurrection as well.

"For the Lord himself will come down from heaven, with a loud command, with the voice of the archangel and with the trumpet call of God, and the dead in Christ will rise first. After that, we who are still alive and are left will be caught up together with them in the clouds to meet the Lord in the air. And so we will be with the Lord forever. Therefore encourage each other with these words" (1 Thess. 4:16–18 NIV).

Job's suffering has been an encouragement to untold millions of men and women who were suffering without a full understanding of why. Job gave them hope that God is aware and is working something of great value through our suffering. Even though Job didn't know the meaning of his suffering, he uttered these words: "Though he slay me, yet will I hope in him" (Job 13:15 NIV).

Through the life of Job, we see that suffering has purpose in the sight of God, and knowing suffering has purpose helps us to endure it. Job asked three questions that point us to a Savior to come and give us hope that is far beyond the temporal, physical suffering of Job. We have hope for an eternal future. But even more meaningful, Job gives us a picture of Christ to come: One who would suffer unjustly at the hands of His enemy (Satan) yet would remain faithful. Because of this, new life would come to the family that would be born out of His victory.

Job's suffering, which God allowed, was the greatest good for the greatest number and for the longest period.

SUFFERINGS OF JOSEPH

Genesis 37–50 tells us the story of Joseph. It is a riveting story of a young boy born as the eleventh of twelve brothers; yet because he was born to his father's (Jacob) favorite wife (Rachel), his father favored him over his older brothers. He was given a coat of many colors, which made his father's preference for him visible to all and began a lifetime of strife between him and his brothers.

One characteristic of the Bible is that it makes no attempt to spruce up its heroes. This was a blatant judgment error on Jacob's part, and it created unnecessary strife in his family. But the Bible records it, because God was going to redeem it.

Joseph was also given dreams that suggest his brothers, father, and mother would one day bow down to him. It is no surprise that one day, when Joseph was far from home and alone with his brothers in the field, they decided to kill him. After some discussion, the compromise was to sell Joseph into slavery. He was then taken to Egypt, and Potiphar, one of Pharaoh's officials (Gen. 39), purchased him.

The story gets worse. After Joseph did impeccable service for Potiphar, Potiphar's wife falsely accuses Joseph of sexual misconduct, and Joseph was sent to prison. Even when he was in prison, God seemingly forgot Joseph until one day when he was miraculously elevated to second in charge of all Egypt because of his ability to interpret Pharaoh's dream and suggest a plan to manage the dream's foreboding prediction.

Now, why would God allow the pain and suffering to fall on a young boy, who by most measures was a good person (although we will discuss more later about who is really good)? If we roll the story ahead, we discover that a great famine came over the land, and Joseph managed the wealth of Egypt to prepare and care for the inhabitants of Egypt and the surrounding nations. Jacob and his sons were in one of those nations and sought the help of Egypt to keep them from starvation. When Joseph and his brothers reunited, and the deceitful brothers were overcome with fear that he might exact revenge on them, he comforted them with these words: "You intended to harm me, but God intended it for good to accomplish what is now being done, the saving of many lives" (Gen. 50:20 NIV).

Jacob and his family were brought to Egypt, where they were cared for while they grew into a nation, a people through whom the Savior of the world would come.

Joseph's suffering not only paved the way for his family's deliverance from physical death but also was part of a master plan to provide deliverance for the world from spiritual death. It was the greatest good for the greatest number and for the longest period.

EXTERMINATION OF THE CANAANITES

We have seen that whether God acts directly (creation) or indirectly (Job and Joseph), He brings about the most good for the greatest number and for the longest period. Now let's examine an entirely different test of God's actions. What about God acting directly to destroy a people group from the face of the earth? "However, in the cities of the nations the Lord your God is giving you as an inheritance, do not leave alive anything that breathes. Completely destroy them–the Hittites, Amorites, Canaanites, Perizzites, Hivites and Jebusites–as the Lord your God has commanded you" (Deut. 20:16–17 NIV).

What about the women and innocent children involved? Were there no "good" people among the Canaanites that God should spare them? What great good could this bring about?

Let's recall that God had already destroyed two groups of people in history before this period: the people of Noah's day who didn't enter the ark and the people of Sodom and Gomorrah. In both cases, God could find no one righteous to spare from His judgment, and in both cases God provided an escape from the coming judgment for those who wanted it.

The people in Noah's day saw him building the ark for almost one hundred years. They saw him and the animals enter the ark—a visibly divine event as far as the animals go—and they saw the clouds gather and the rain come. Yet there is no mention in scripture of anyone banging on the side of the ark (as the movies depict), begging to be let in as the waters rose.

The attending angels directly offered escape to Lot's sons-in-law, but they refused. The people of Sodom saw the power of the angels when some were struck blind, but they took no heed, and they perished. So what about the Canaanites? Were they as depraved as the preflood and Sodom and Gomorrah cultures?

Four hundred years before God gave the Israelites the command to go and destroy the Canaanites, He said this to Abraham, who was living in Canaan at the time: "Then the Lord said to him, 'Know for certain that your descendants will be strangers in a country not their own, and they will be enslaved and mistreated four hundred years. But I will punish the nation they serve as slaves, and afterward they will come out with great possessions. You, however, will go to your fathers in peace and be buried at a good old age. In the fourth generation your descendants will come back here, for the sin of the Amorites (Canaanites) has not yet reached its full measure'" (Gen. 15:13–16 NIV).

God had waited four hundred years to bring judgment on the Canaanites. They were guilty of despicable practices, including burning their own children to death in sacrifice to their gods. Leviticus 18:1–20:27 lists the deeds of the Canaanites as practices the children of Israel must avoid. It is also clear the Canaanites knew judgment was coming and that God was with Israel based on this statement from Rahab before Jericho was destroyed: "And said to them, 'I know that the Lord has given this land to you and that a great fear of you has fallen on us, so that all who live in this country are melting in fear because of you'" (Josh. 2:9 NIV).

So they had been warned. God waited four hundred years for them to reform their cultures. He promised destruction through Abraham while living in Canaan, which he no doubt shared with them, and God provided a means of escape. Rahab is a great example of how any who wanted to escape would be provided the way out.

But why kill all of them? Deuteronomy 9:1–6 gives God's rationale for their extermination. "After the Lord your God has driven them out before you, do not say to yourself, 'The Lord has brought me here to take possession of this land because of my righteousness.' No, it is on account of the wickedness of these nations that the Lord is going to drive them out before you" (Deut. 9:4 NIV).

Like the people of Noah's day and the people of Sodom and Gomorrah, the Canaanites had become a people in whom there was no hope of redemption. Their children were being born into a culture that was so depraved, they were without hope of repentance, and they were bent on the destruction of the Jews, through whom the Savior of the world would come? "Otherwise, they will teach you to follow all the detestable things they do in worshiping their gods, and you will sin against the Lord your God" (Deut. 20:18 NIV).

God's priority is the most saved, the fewest lost; and the most good for the greatest number for the longest period. The Canaanites had become a clear and present danger to both ideas. We see an example of this when Samuel told Saul to completely destroy the Amalekites (1 Sam. 15:3). Instead, Saul spared Agag, their king, and failed to accomplish the task of killing all the Amalekites. How do we know? Because an Agagite showed up centuries later in the story of Esther (Haman), and he made every effort to destroy the Jewish people in exile there—the very people from whom the Savior, Jesus, would come.

Centuries later, after God had removed the Israelites from the land because they had committed many of the same sins as the Canaanites, God promised to bring them back again and said this through Ezekiel: "No longer will the people of Israel have malicious neighbors who are painful briers and sharp thorns. Then they will know that I am the Sovereign Lord" (Ezek. 28:24 NIV).

God knew what He was doing when He ordered the mass destruction of the Canaanites. Was God's command moral?

We are quick to impose our morality on God when God has attributes we don't. How does this matter? Could it ever be moral to pass on a two-lane highway while approaching the crest of a hill? It certainly wouldn't be legal in most states I know, but the question is, could it ever be moral? What if you could see the other side of the hill and knew there were no cars approaching? It would still be illegal to make the pass, but it would no longer be immoral because you would be imposing no danger or risk to yourself or anyone else.

Omniscience gives God the ability to act in ways that may appear immoral to us but are perfectly moral—something done in the best interest of all people, including those who might have to suffer.

God knew the Canaanites represented a real and long-term threat to His plan to bring a Savior into the world through Israel. He knew they were depraved beyond reversal. He provided four hundred years of warning before their destruction, and He provided a way out for those who desired it. And from this action, we see Israel established as a nation, protected in exile in Babylon, and returned to the land where the Savior was born centuries later—the greatest blessing the world has ever known.

The destruction of the Canaanites was a direct act of God, and it was tragic that a civilization reached the depraved state that the inhabitants of Canaan did. But God couldn't allow that culture to corrupt and destroy other cultures, especially the people through whom the world's greatest gift was to come. There was a cancer in the world. God removed it, and that act resulted in the most good for the greatest number and for the longest period.

CRUCIFIXION OF JESUS

> When they had crucified him, they divided up his clothes by casting lots. (Matt. 27:35 NIV)

> It was the third hour when they crucified him. (Mark 15:25–26 NIV)

> When they came to the place called the Skull, there they crucified him, along with the criminals—one on his right, the other on his left. (Luke 23:33 NIV)

> For to be sure, he was crucified in weakness, yet he lives by God's power. (2 Cor. 13:4 NIV)

One of the most heinous events in human history (perhaps *the* most heinous) was not only planned and allowed by God; it also happened to God.

The only man to ever live a perfect life, keep the law of the prophets exactly, and remain in constant fellowship with God was betrayed by a friend. He was falsely accused at a sham trial by the religious leaders of His day, turned over to a cruel Roman government, and nearly flogged to death. Then he suffered the worst death known to man at that time: crucifixion.

Why did God allow this? How did this result in the most good for the greatest number and for the longest period?

I'm not going to present here the evidence for the crucifixion of Jesus. Many other authors have provided more than sufficient evidence from both secular and Jewish historians that the event occurred. Assuming it did, how could it be of the greatest benefit to so many for so long?

One question I have discovered many Christians are unable to answer is, why did Jesus have to die? Why couldn't God just forgive us all for our sins?

God has made it clear since Adam and Eve sinned in the garden that the only way sinful man can stand before a holy God is with a divinely provided garment at the cost of shed blood (Gen. 3:21). Sin was and is a serious matter to God. For Him to simply forgive would leave Him guilty of injustice. And if God punished us all for our sin as we deserve, by death, He wouldn't be merciful. Yet He is a God of mercy and justice. How could God show mercy to us for our transgressions and still be just?

God set a pattern for what He was going to do when He spared Isaac and promised to provide a sacrifice, and when He instructed the Hebrews to spread blood on their doorposts to protect them from the angel of death, which would visit Egypt on the night of the Passover. He further advanced this imagery by establishing the sacrificial system when the tabernacle in the wilderness was built. All these events pointed to the ultimate sacrifice; a God-man would volunteer His life as a one-time sacrifice for all people sufficient to absolve anyone's sins who would accept this sacrifice through repentance and perseverance.

One person, even if he or she lived a perfect life, couldn't die for the sins of all people—perhaps only for the sins of another person— but a God-man could die for everyone's sins. And Jesus, God the Son, willingly took our place in submission to the Father to be that sacrifice. "Pilate said, 'Don't you realize I have power either to free you or to crucify you?' Jesus answered, 'You would have no power over me if it were not given to you from above'" (John 19:10–11 NIV).

Jesus was crucified, and all men from all time who wished to have their sins removed could be exonerated because God assumed their guilt and took their punishment; it is His gift to us at great cost to Him. Jesus had to die so God could show us mercy, even grace, and still be just. And this was absolutely the greatest good for the greatest number and for the longest period.

RESURRECTION OF JESUS

> Jesus said to her, "I am the resurrection and the life. He who believes in me will live, even though he dies; and whoever lives and believes in me will never die." (John 11:25–26 NIV)

> The Son of Man must be delivered into the hands of sinful men, be crucified and on the third day be raised again. (Luke 24:7 NIV)

Many people find belief in the resurrection of Jesus to be a preposterous claim. For this very reason, if Jesus was resurrected, it is a unique happening in history and demands that His teachings be given higher authority than anyone before or after Him.

I won't engage in an apologetic for the resurrection of Jesus here. As with the crucifixion, many others have done so using references to both secular and Jewish historians. I will offer this observation that I believe gives great credibility to this claim. Almost all biblical scholars agree that the New Testament was written in the lifetime of eyewitnesses to the crucifixion and resurrection of Jesus. But there is also a very strong case for the fact that the New Testament was all written before AD 70. Why? Because a Roman army, led by the future Roman emperor Titus, destroyed the temple in AD 70. Jesus foresaw the destruction of the temple in Matthew 24:1–2.

"Jesus left the temple and was walking away when his disciples came up to him to call his attention to its buildings. 'Do you see all these things?' he asked. 'I tell you the truth, not one stone here will be left on another; every one will be thrown down'" (Matt. 24:1–2 NIV).

It's more than reasonable to assume that any writing about the teachings of Jesus after AD 70 would have certainly referred to this event as an example of His authority as a prophet. Yet none of the books of the New Testament refer to this event. Why is this important?

President John Kennedy was assassinated in 1963 when I was eleven years old. Many of my peers, parents, and I vividly remember the day—and that was over fifty years ago. If someone were to claim today that President Kennedy had resurrected from the dead, performed miracles, or made any other such outlandish claims, there would be an outcry of denial from all the living eyewitnesses to his life and death.

Likewise, the temple in Jerusalem was destroyed less than forty years after Jesus's death and resurrection, and with all the books written about Jesus's life, death, resurrection, and miraculous acts, there would surely have been many who were witnesses of these events to write rebuttals of these claims—yet there are none by the eyewitnesses.

Why then is the resurrection important? Couldn't Christianity still survive without this event being true? The resurrection is of infinite importance, and no, Christianity depends entirely on the resurrection of Christ for its veracity. Paul said this succinctly in his first letter to the Corinthians. "And if Christ has not been raised, your faith is futile; you are still in your sins. Then those also who have fallen asleep in Christ are lost. If only for this life we have hope in Christ, we are to be pitied more than all men" (1 Cor. 15:17–19 NIV).

Jesus's resurrection was the validation of His claims to be both God and Savior to all men.

> Jesus answered them, "Destroy this temple, and I will raise it again in three days." (John 2:19 NIV)

> After he was raised from the dead, his disciples recalled what he had said. Then they believed the Scripture and the words that Jesus had spoken. (John 2:22 NIV)

Because He predicted His own death and resurrection—and was indeed resurrected—He can be trusted in all He claimed, including who He claimed to be. And this means the resurrection was the greatest good for the greatest number and for the longest period.

Let's move on to our next megatheme. How does God accomplish His purposes in the world?

MEGATHEME 3:

GOD ACCOMPLISHES HIS PURPOSES THROUGH THE FREE CHOICES OF MEN AND WOMEN

A few years back, I was asked to speak at an adult discipleship seminar. To open the session, an elderly (and I am sure much-respected) member of the class opened the meeting by asking for prayer concerns. Then, just before he prayed, he said, "Well, we all know God is going to do what God is going to do, but let's pray anyway." *Wow*, I thought. *Does this man really believe that?*

There are many truths of scripture that seem to be a paradox yet need to be held in tension. I call these the "both ands" of scripture. For example:

1. God is *both* one being *and* three persons (centers of consciousness).
2. Jesus is *both* fully human *and* fully God (the second person of the Trinity).
3. God is *both* transcendent (existing apart from and not subject to the limitations of the material universe) *and* immanent (permanently pervading and sustaining the universe).
4. *Both* God *and* man authored the Bible.
5. Salvation is *both* by grace *and* confirmed by works.
6. Salvation is *both* eternally secure *and* a gift to those who persevere.
7. We are *both* justified *and* in the process of being sanctified.

I could go on, but the "both and" we want to consider in this megatheme is "God is sovereign, and man is free." Both statements are true at all times and in every situation.

The "both ands" above are in tension with one another. Our temptation is to try to resolve the tension by making one statement truer than the other or emphasizing one at the expense of diminishing the other. To do this will lead one into theological error. God is sovereign. His purposes will prevail as the elderly man correctly stated; however, we are free to choose what we will do today, and those choices matter, including the choice to pray. We live in a world where God accomplishes His purposes through the free choices of men and women.

First, here some passages on the sovereignty of God and the free will of people: "Indeed Herod and Pontius Pilate met together with the Gentiles and the people of Israel in this city to conspire against your holy servant Jesus, whom you anointed. They did what your power and will had decided beforehand should happen" (Acts 4:27–28 NIV).

Men used their free choices to meet and conspire against Jesus, but God used their free choices for His purpose. "Here I am! I stand at the door and knock. If anyone hears my voice and opens the door, I will come in and eat with him, and he with me" (Rev. 3:20 NIV).

Jesus saves those who hear Him and act on His calling. This passage would be meaningless if we didn't have the ability (freedom) to hear and respond. "For those God foreknew he also predestined to be conformed to the likeness of his Son, that he might be the firstborn among many brothers" (Rom. 8:29 NIV).

This passage says God uses His omniscience, His foreknowledge of events, and our responses to those events to select (predestine) us for salvation. "This is what the Lord says: 'When seventy years are completed for Babylon, I will come to you and fulfill my gracious promise to bring you back to this place. For I know the plans I have for you,' declares the Lord, 'plans to prosper you and not to harm you, plans to give you hope and a future. Then you will call upon me and come and pray to me, and I will listen to you'" (Jer. 29:10–12 NIV).

God had specific reasons for waiting seventy years to return the Israelites to their homeland from their exile in Babylon; but one of those reasons was that it would take seventy years for the Jews to finally "call upon me and … pray to me." God foreknew that Israel would take seventy years to repent and call on Him before He planned their release from exile. Our prayers do matter. God works through our prayers to accomplish His purposes.

> And everyone who calls
> on the name of the Lord will be saved;
> for on Mount Zion and in Jerusalem
> there will be deliverance,
> as the Lord has said,
> among the survivors
> whom the Lord calls.
> (Joel 2:32 NIV)

Here we see both truths at work. Men are free to choose ("everyone who calls on the name of the Lord"), and God has already chosen ("the survivors whom [He] calls"). God is sovereign, and men are free.

Here are some specific examples of men's choices and God's purposes working in harmony. Held in tension, both operate fully and without restraint yet accomplish God's purposes.

PHARAOH AND THE RELEASE OF THE ISRAELITES FROM EGYPT

Whenever I say, "God works through the free choices of men and women," one of the first objections I hear is, What about Pharaoh and how God hardened his heart? "The Lord said to Moses, 'When you return to Egypt, see that you perform before Pharaoh all the wonders I have given you the power to do. But I will harden his heart so that he will not let the people go'" (Ex. 4:21 NIV).

Who hardened Pharaoh's heart? There are fourteen clauses where God takes responsibility for Pharaoh's decision, four clauses where the language doesn't tell us who takes responsibility, and thirty-five clauses where Pharaoh takes responsibility for his own decision. It would appear that both God and Pharaoh were doing the hardening. But how can this be?

Ultimately, God designed and built our consciences. Our consciences are designed to become less sensitive to disobedience (sin) as we ignore their promptings. When we disobey, our consciences become seared, calloused, or hardened. Who then is hardening our heart? Both us (through our free choices) and God (who built the very mechanism that hardens during repeated refusals to ignore its warning).

So Pharaoh made free choices to reject Moses's warnings about holding the Israelites in slavery in Egypt. But God, knowing Pharaoh would make these choices, planned a strategy to use Pharaoh's choices to demonstrate His power over all the Egyptian gods and secure the release of the Israelites from Egypt.

JOSEPH'S BECOMING SECOND TO PHARAOH IN EGYPT

God had a plan for Joseph to become second in power to Pharaoh, a position we will call "prime minister." Why? Joseph could provide for Jacob and his sons (the infant nation of Israel, the people through whom the promised Savior would come) during a time of extreme famine.

How Joseph rose to the position of prime minister is an astounding sequence of free choices by men and women.

- His brothers decide to kill him out of envy, but instead they sold him to a passing caravan to be sold as a slave.
- Potiphar chose him as a slave and took him into his house, eventually giving him authority over all his affairs.
- Potiphar's wife tried to seduce him and falsely accused him of sexual misconduct.
- Potiphar had him thrown into prison where he again rose to be in charge of many prison activities and prisoners.

- Pharaoh had a dream, and a former prisoner remembered that Joseph had a gift for interpreting dreams.
- Pharaoh called for a slave to interpret his dream (think on that one for a moment), then promoted that slave to the position of prime minister of Egypt.

Only God could use the free choices of men and women to accomplish His purposes. And we know God foresaw this because of the dreams Joseph had of his brothers, father, and mother bowing down to him, the very dreams that were the source of the envy that kicked off the sequence of free choices to make him second-in-command of Egypt.

ESTHER'S RESCUE OF THE JEWS FROM HAMAN

In a story that never mentions God by name, we see God's handiwork everywhere. A vile Agagite, Haman, was a close adviser to King Xerxes, and because of the contempt his people had toward the Jews, he wanted to see their extinction. You may remember that Saul was ordered to destroy all the Amalekites but spared their king (Agag). Now we see that others escaped as well because here was one of their descendants, and Haman demonstrated the reason God ordered their destruction, their unmitigated contempt for the Jewish people.

Through a series of free human choices, God's plan for the salvation of the Jews was executed.

- A queen refused to allow her husband, the king, to put her on display in front of his banquet guests.
- The queen was deposed, and a new queen was sought to replace her.
- The king chose Esther of Jewish descent.
- Esther's uncle, Mordecai, saved the king's life earlier by alerting the king's guard of some potential assassins.

- Haman knew Mordecai and despised him, prompting him to hatch a plan to kill Mordecai and exterminate the Jews throughout the kingdom.
- Haman got the king to sign an order that would result in the Jews' extermination.
- Mordecai convinced Esther to intercede for her people at risk of her own life.
- Esther alerted the king to Haman's treachery against her and her people.
- Haman falls on the queen to beg her intercession to spare him from the king's wrath.
- The king ordered Haman killed on the gallows he had prepared for Mordecai.
- The king signed a new order, allowing the Jews to defend themselves against anyone who acted on his first order, thus sparing their lives.

Now all these events hinged on one particular evening, when the king had trouble sleeping. He called for his historic records that he might read them—no doubt to help put him to sleep. He just "happened" to read in these records that Mordecai had previously spared his life and had never been recognized for his service. This began his favorable disposition toward Mordecai, which ultimately led to Mordecai's becoming an adviser to the king and intercessor for the Jews.

All these events happened through the free choices of human beings, yet God's plan was perfectly executed.

JONAH'S MINISTRY TO THE PEOPLE OF NINEVEH

Does God ever interfere with our choices or even coerce them toward His purposes? People often point to Jonah as an example of God's forced or coerced decision-making.

Commanded to go preach repentance to his enemies (the

Assyrians in Nineveh), Jonah didn't want to do this. Deciding to run from God's command, Jonah boarded a ship and encountered a storm at sea. He recognized he was the cause of the storm, and he volunteered to be cast overboard, where a great fish swallowed him. In the belly of the fish, he repented and went to speak to the Ninevites, who repented and were spared God's judgment.

Did God bring unpleasant circumstances on Jonah because of his disobedience? Yes, He did. Did God force Jonah's will in the matter? This is not a story of God coercing or forcing someone's will; this is a story of a merciful, even gracious, God offering a second chance.

God didn't force Jonah's decision. God told him what to do; Jonah freely chose to disobey, and God could have let him go his way and perish apart from Him. Instead, God disciplined him for the wrong decision and gave him a second opportunity to make a different one. I don't find this troubling. I welcome God's discipline when I'm straying from His purposes. God knows my heart's desire isn't to stray. Through discipline, God actually grants me what I want most: a heart and attitudes that please Him.

The book of Jonah doesn't reflect well on him. He was still angry at the end of the book at the mercy God showed his enemy. However, Jonah wrote this book and exposed his arrogance and pride in this matter. This was a great act of humility, which would suggest that later, Jonah was glad God intervened in his disobedience so he might learn to be a better servant and prophet. God did intervene and gave Jonah a gift he hadn't yet asked for but had great need of: humility.

God accomplished His purpose for the Ninevites and for Jonah through Jonah's free choices. A very similar argument could be made for Saul of Tarsus and his experience on the road to Damascus.

MOUNT MORIAH AND CALVARY

The last example I offer is perhaps the most extraordinary one. Millions of people's free choices, spanning over two thousand years, brought about an event exactly as God had foretold and purposed.

Two thousand years before Christ's death, God asked the patriarch Abraham to sacrifice his son Isaac on Mount Moriah. "Then God said, 'Take your son, your only son, Isaac, whom you love, and go to the region of Moriah. Sacrifice him there as a burnt offering on one of the mountains I will tell you about'" (Gen. 22:2 NIV).

Now, explaining why God told Abraham to do this isn't the purpose of this section. But the fact that God told Abraham to go to Moriah is. The topography of Moriah is flat on the southern end and rises to a peak on the northern end. While the scriptures don't tell us exactly where on Moriah's top Abraham went to offer Isaac, it's a reasonable assumption that he went to the highest point, the northern end, because this was the custom of the day for offering a sacrifice to one's god.

While going up the mountain, Isaac asked, "Where is the lamb for the sacrifice?" "Abraham answered, 'God himself will provide the lamb for the burnt offering, my son.' And the two of them went on together" (Gen. 22:8 NIV).

After God provided the ram for Abraham to sacrifice, we read, "So Abraham called that place The Lord Will Provide. And to this day it is said, 'On the mountain of the Lord it will be provided'" (Gen. 22:14 NIV).

God didn't require Abraham's son as a sacrifice that day but provided the sacrifice and named the location "The Lord Will Provide."

Roll the clock ahead to David's census, which displeased God. To appease God's wrath, David was ordered to build an altar on the threshing floor of Araunah the Jebusite. "Then the angel of the Lord ordered Gad to tell David to go up and build an altar to the Lord on the threshing floor of Araunah the Jebusite" (1 Chron. 21:18 NIV).

When David did this, he saw the Angel of the Lord sheath his sword because God's wrath was appeased. "Then the Lord spoke to the angel, and he put his sword back into its sheath" (1 Chron. 21:27 NIV).

David's response was this: "Then David said, 'The house of the

Lord God is to be here, and also the altar of burnt offering for Israel'" (1 Chron. 22:1 NIV).

Why is this important? Because Solomon built the temple where his father David had instructed: at the threshing floor of Araunah, which was on Mount Moriah. "Then Solomon began to build the temple of the Lord in Jerusalem on Mount Moriah, where the Lord had appeared to his father David. It was on the threshing floor of Araunah the Jebusite, the place provided by David" (2 Chron. 3:1 NIV).

If Moriah was flat on one end and steep on the other, where would one build a structure like the temple? Logically the answer is on the southern end. Solomon's temple was built there, but Nebuchadnezzar II destroyed it in 587 BC. Zerubbabel rebuilt it in 515 BC, and Herod improved on it in 19 BC. This was the temple that stood in Jesus's day.

Over two thousand years since Abraham scaled Moriah, the northern end of Moriah had become worn by the weather and presented a bald peak the Romans had chosen for executions because the gruesome scene could be seen for many miles. The peak was named the "place of the skull" or Golgotha.

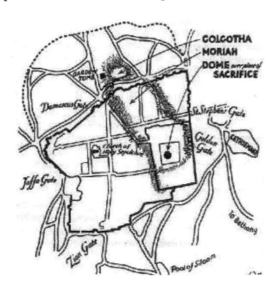

Yes, it is highly probable that the very place God told Abraham, "I will provide a sacrifice"—the very place God spared Abraham's son—is where He didn't spare His Son and did provide the sacrificial lamb. His own Son satisfied His wrath against the sins of mankind (sheathing His sword).

Millions of free choices of men and women occurred during this two-thousand-year span, yet God's plan to provide the ultimate sacrifice, sufficient for the sins of all men and women for all time, was accomplished. Christ died where Isaac had been spared.

Only a truly sovereign God can give us complete freedom of choice and still accomplish His purposes in our lives. We live in a world where God accomplishes His purposes through the free choices of men and women.

DISOBEDIENCE (SIN) IS DESTRUCTIVE

In this chapter we will look at some megathemes that speak to the destructive nature of sin and the consequences of our obedience or disobedience to God's word.

MEGATHEME 4:

WE MISS GOD'S BEST THROUGH DISOBEDIENCE

I have, on more than one occasion, listened to others explain why the course of action they were about to take was good for them, even though scripture spoke plainly against it. I have responded in each case with this: "You are about to bring consequences on you and those you love that God never intended you to bear."

How do I know this? Because scripture is clear that we miss God's best for our lives (and those in our sphere of influence) through disobedience. Here are some passages that address this megatheme:

> The Lord saw how great man's wickedness on the earth had become, and that every inclination of the thoughts of his heart was only evil all the time. The Lord was grieved that he had made man on the earth, and his heart was filled with pain. So the Lord said, "I will wipe mankind, whom I have created, from the

face of the earth—men and animals, and creatures that move along the ground, and birds of the air—for I am grieved that I have made them." (Gen. 6:5–7 NIV)

Now if you obey me fully and keep my covenant, then out of all nations you will be my treasured possession. (Ex. 19:5 NIV)

When such a person hears the words of this oath, he invokes a blessing on himself and therefore thinks, "I will be safe, even though I persist in going my own way." This will bring disaster on the watered land as well as the dry. (Deut. 29:19 NIV)

"I have not made trouble for Israel," Elijah replied. "But you and your father's family have. You have abandoned the Lord's commands and have followed the Baals." (1 Kings 18:18 NIV)

But your iniquities have separated you from your God; your sins have hidden his face from you, so that he will not hear. (Isa. 59:2 NIV)

And if at another time I announce that a nation or kingdom is to be built up and planted, and if it does evil in my sight and does not obey me, then I will reconsider the good I had intended to do for it. (Jer. 18:9–10 NIV)

"For I know the plans I have for you," declares the Lord, "plans to prosper you and not to harm you, plans to give you hope and a future." (Jer. 29:11 NIV)

"Do not my words do good to him whose ways are upright?" (Mic. 2:7 NIV)

And these are just a few verses that speak not only about God's plans to do good to us but also about the fact that He reconsiders the good He intended for us. Also, our disobedience brings "disaster on the watered land as well as the dry," meaning that everyone in our sphere of influence (the guilty and the innocent) can suffer for our disobedience.

Let's consider some specific examples of this truth.

ABRAHAM'S LACK OF PATIENCE FOR SARAH TO PRODUCE AN HEIR

God had clearly told Abraham that he would have an heir. Genesis 15:4 (NIV) says, "Then the word of the Lord came to him: 'This man will not be your heir, but a son coming from your own body will be your heir.'"

After living in Canaan for ten years, Sarah, his wife, had borne him no children, and she suggested that he take her maidservant Hagar as a way he could have an heir. Abraham agreed. Now Abraham's walk with God was a work in progress, and it would become much more steadfast than what he demonstrated here. Because of Abraham's disobedience, his family and their descendants would suffer for millennia, even to this day.

The strife in his family began almost immediately with Sarah's resentment toward Hagar and Ishmael (the child of the union of Abram [Abraham] with Sarai's [Sarah's] maidservant Hagar). And when Isaac, the son of promise was born, even greater resentment occurred to the point that Abraham had to send Hagar and Ishmael away into the care of God. This strife continues today; descendants of Ishmael and Isaac are contending to be the rightful heir of Abraham.

THE DISOBEDIENCE OF JACOB'S OLDEST THREE SONS: REUBEN, LEVI, AND SIMEON

It was the practice in antiquity for a father to pass his greatest blessing to his firstborn son. This was not only his wealth and possessions but also any promises given to him, and they were referred to as the "birthright."

Jacob knew this was important because he knew of the promise given to Abraham and his father, Isaac. He was second born and desired the birthright his brother, Esau, was entitled to. Through trickery, he stole Esau's birthright.

Genesis 25:31–34 (NIV) says, "Jacob replied, 'First sell me your birthright.' 'Look, I am about to die,' Esau said. 'What good is the birthright to me?' But Jacob said, 'Swear to me first.' So he swore an oath to him, selling his birthright to Jacob. Then Jacob gave Esau some bread and some lentil stew. He ate and drank, and then got up and left. So Esau despised his birthright."

And with more trickery and his mother's help, Jacob got his father, Isaac, to bless him with the birthright.

Genesis 27:22–23 (NIV) says, "Jacob went close to his father Isaac, who touched him and said, 'The voice is the voice of Jacob, but the hands are the hands of Esau.' He did not recognize him, for his hands were hairy like those of his brother Esau; so he blessed him."

Jacob's oldest son, Reuben, slept with his father's concubine Bilhah, the mother of Dan and Naphtali. Genesis 35:22 (NIV) says, "While Israel was living in that region, Reuben went in and slept with his father's concubine Bilhah, and Israel heard of it."

Jacob's next two sons, Simeon and Levi, broke an agreement Jacob had made with a neighbor, Hamor. Hamor's son Shechem had raped Dinah, the daughter of Leah (Jacob's first wife) and sister of Simeon and Levi. Hamor brought his son to Jacob and asked permission for Shechem to marry Dinah, for he loved her. An agreement was struck that this could happen if all the men in Hamor's city were circumcised. Hamor agreed. But Simeon and Levi intended to use the deal to exact their revenge.

Genesis 34:25 (NIV) says "Three days later, while all of them were still in pain, two of Jacob's sons, Simeon and Levi, Dinah's brothers, took their swords and attacked the unsuspecting city, killing every male."

Reuben defiled his father's concubine; Simeon and Levi defiled their father's word. As a result, all three lost out on the most precious thing their father had to give them: a birthright blessing. The blessing Jacob gave to Judah best describes the opportunity the older three brothers missed through their disobedience. Genesis 49:8–10 (NIV) says,

> Judah, your brothers will praise you;
> your hand will be on the neck of your enemies;
> your father's sons will bow down to you.
> You are a lion's cub, O Judah;
> you return from the prey, my son.
> Like a lion he crouches and lies down,
> like a lioness—who dares to rouse him?
> The scepter will not depart from Judah,
> nor the ruler's staff from between his feet,
> until he comes to whom it belongs
> and the obedience of the nations is his.

Judah wasn't without fault. He had slept with his daughter-in-law Tamar because she had disguised herself as a prostitute to make him perform his duties as a kinsman-redeemer after her husband died. (This required Judah to give Tamar one of his other sons as a husband or become a husband to her himself so she would not be disgraced by bearing no son to carry on the name of her dead husband.)

But Judah had a couple of noble moments, giving us a glimpse of Christ to come. First, Judah interceded for Joseph to prevent the older brothers from killing him and suggested he be sold into slavery. And after the brothers' first encounter with Joseph (whom they didn't recognize) in Egypt, they were sent home to bring Benjamin back. Jacob refused to let Benjamin go for fear he and his brothers would be killed in Egypt. But Judah stood in the gap for Benjamin and his brothers. Genesis 43:8–9 (NIV) says, "Then Judah said to Israel his father, 'Send the boy along with me and we will go at once, so that we and you and our children may live and not die. I myself will guarantee his safety; you can hold me personally responsible for him.

If I do not bring him back to you and set him here before you, I will bear the blame before you all my life.'"

Judah demonstrated who Christ would be, one who stands in the gap by volunteering to redeem his brothers or forever bear the blame. Then, in the presence of Joseph when he (Joseph) asked the brothers to leave Benjamin with him and go back to their father, Judah interceded for Benjamin and said, "Now then, please let your servant remain here as my lord's slave in place of the boy, and let the boy return with his brothers. How can I go back to my father if the boy is not with me? No! Do not let me see the misery that would come upon my father" (Gen. 44:33–34 NIV).

Judah offered himself in place of Benjamin as substitutionary atonement, a type of Christ. Christ would come through Judah's lineage, but Reuben, Simeon, and Levi missed out on this blessing through disobedience.

THE DISOBEDIENCE OF MOSES

Scripture says Moses was one of the humblest men on earth. "(Now Moses was a very humble man, more humble than anyone else on the face of the earth)" (Num. 12:3 NIV).

He had been carrying out God's commands flawlessly in his quest to lead them out of Egypt and into the wilderness in preparation for going into Canaan. On one occasion, when the children of Israel complained about lack of water, God commanded him to strike a rock, and when he did, water gushed forth.

But on a later occasion, when the Israelites again complained about their lack of water, God told Moses to "speak to the rock." Instead, Moses did something else. "He and Aaron gathered the assembly together in front of the rock and Moses said to them, 'Listen, you rebels, must we bring you water out of this rock?' Then Moses raised his arm and struck the rock twice with his staff. Water gushed out, and the community and their livestock drank" (Num. 20:10–11 NIV).

Notice the frustration in Moses's voice and the statement "Must *we* bring you water" (emphasis mine)? In a moment of weakness, not only did he not do as God had asked, but he even presented himself as coregent with God to provide for the people's needs. God responds this way: "But the Lord said to Moses and Aaron, 'Because you did not trust in me enough to honor me as holy in the sight of the Israelites, you will not bring this community into the land I give them'" (Num. 20:12 NIV).

If Moses, after living a life of incredible humility and obedience, could suffer consequences for one disobedient act, then we too may also miss God's best through our disobedience.

ISRAEL'S DISOBEDIENCE IN THE DESERT

After arriving at Mount Sinai in the desert, Moses ascended the mountain to receive God's instructions for the people of Israel. God had already demonstrated His power and authority to the Israelites in their release from Egypt and salvation from Pharaoh's army. Moses was on the mountain for some time, receiving the Ten Commandments and many other instructions. Then something happened. "When the people saw that Moses was so long in coming down from the mountain, they gathered around Aaron and said, 'Come, make us gods who will go before us. As for this fellow Moses who brought us up out of Egypt, we don't know what has happened to him'" (Ex. 32:1 NIV).

How quickly they forgot the demonstrations of the power of their God and wanted to revert to idol worship (the gods of Egypt). They made a golden calf and worshipped it.

God informed Moses of this development and expressed His desire to destroy them all. Moses interceded for the people, and God relented. When Moses arrived at the camp and confronted the people, he called for those who were for the Lord, and the Levites came to him. He sent the Levites throughout the camp to kill those who were leaders in committing this detestable offense before God. The Levites killed about three thousand Israelites that day.

Moses was still unsure that God's wrath had been appeased, so he went before God to offer atonement for the people's sin. God replied, "Now go, lead the people to the place I spoke of, and my angel will go before you. However, when the time comes for me to punish, I will punish them for their sin" (Ex. 32:34 NIV).

And scripture further says, "And the Lord struck the people with a plague because of what they did with the calf Aaron had made" (Ex. 32:35 NIV). Disobedience has consequences.

SAUL'S DISOBEDIENCE AT GILGAL

God chose Saul to be the first king of Israel. "Then Samuel took a flask of oil and poured it on Saul's head and kissed him, saying, 'Has not the Lord anointed you leader over his inheritance?'" (1 Sam. 10:1 NIV).

God came upon Saul in power and with great favor. "The Spirit of the Lord will come upon you in power, and you will prophesy with them; and you will be changed into a different person" (1 Sam. 10:6 NIV).

But when Saul's first test of obedience came, he failed miserably: Samuel gave him these instructions: "Go down ahead of me to Gilgal. I will surely come down to you to sacrifice burnt offerings and fellowship offerings, but you must wait seven days until I come to you and tell you what you are to do" (1 Sam. 10:8 NIV).

Saul went to Gilgal and began to assemble his army to fight against the Philistines, who were growing stronger by the day and amassing their forces. "The Philistines assembled to fight Israel, with three thousand chariots, six thousand charioteers, and soldiers as numerous as the sand on the seashore. They went up and camped at Micmash, east of Beth Aven" (1 Sam. 13:5 NIV).

Saul grew impatient while waiting for Samuel. He thought he should attack the Philistines as soon as possible before they could muster more troops. So he took on a duty he hadn't been given. In those days, the office of king and priest was separated; it was split between Saul (king) and Samuel (priest). Saul took on the priestly role as well. "So he said, 'Bring me the burnt offering and the fellowship offerings.' And Saul offered up the burnt offering" (1 Sam. 13:9 NIV).

Immediately after this: "'You acted foolishly,' Samuel said. 'You have not kept the command the Lord your God gave you; if you had, he would have established your kingdom over Israel for all time. But now your kingdom will not endure; the Lord has sought out a man after his own heart and appointed him leader of his people, because you have not kept the Lord's command'" (1 Sam. 13:13–14 NIV).

Saul grew impatient while waiting on the Lord's timing. He took matters into his own hands, which was an affront to God. It's arrogant to assume our plans—our timing—are better than God's. And for this, Saul lost the kingdom; his sons wouldn't inherit the throne. He missed God's best through disobedience.

DAVID'S DISOBEDIENCE WITH URIAH AND BATHSHEBA

This is perhaps one of the best-known stories of the Bible. Israel's greatest king, a "man after God's own heart" (1 Sam. 13:14 NIV), gave into lust and committed adultery with the wife (Bathsheba) of one of his most trusted and loyal generals, Uriah the Hittite. Bathsheba became pregnant, and David conspired with the general of his army (Joab) to have Uriah killed so his sin could go unnoticed.

David thought he had pulled off the deed, but the prophet Nathan, whom God had sent, confronted him. After one of the most piercing rebukes a prophet ever gave a man, Nathan concluded with this: "Now, therefore, the sword will never depart from your house, because you despised me and took the wife of Uriah the Hittite to be your own" (2 Sam. 12:10 NIV).

Conflict, strife, envy, rape, murder, and betrayal became rampant in David's household. Unlike Saul, David did repent, and we have one of the most beautiful passages of repentance in scripture, which documents his repentance (Ps. 51). David's relationship with Yahweh was restored, and no fewer than eight times God referred to David in Isaiah, Jeremiah, and Ezekiel as "my servant David."

This is good news. Despite David's adultery and murder, God restored and revered David as "my servant." The lesson for us is that while there is forgiveness for sins through the substitutionary sacrifice of Christ on the cross, there are still consequences. We miss God's best through disobedience.

SOLOMON'S DISOBEDIENCE REGARDING FOREIGN WIVES

Solomon was another king who was given a great start. But he had an eye for foreign women. God said this about marrying Canaanite women to the Israelites before they entered Canaan: "Do not intermarry with them. Do not give your daughters to their sons or take their daughters for your sons, for they will turn your sons away from following me to serve other gods, and the Lord's anger will burn against you and will quickly destroy you" (Deut. 7:3–4 NIV).

But Solomon disregarded this warning, and we find this recorded about him: "King Solomon, however, loved many foreign women besides Pharaoh's daughter—Moabites, Ammonites, Edomites, Sidonians and Hittites. They were from nations about which the Lord had told the Israelites, 'You must not intermarry with them, because they will surely turn your hearts after their gods.' Nevertheless, Solomon held fast to them in love" (1 Kings 11:1–2 NIV).

Furthermore: "He had seven hundred wives of royal birth and three hundred concubines, and his wives led him astray" (1 Kings 11:3 NIV).

I will later discuss the pattern disobedience follows to lead us into complete destruction if we don't repent. Here we see the result of Solomon's disobedience without repentance: "On a hill east of Jerusalem, Solomon built a high place for Chemosh the detestable god of Moab, and for Molech the detestable god of the Ammonites.

He did the same for all his foreign wives, who burned incense and offered sacrifices to their gods" (1 Kings 11:7–8 NIV).

The story concludes this way: "So the Lord said to Solomon, 'Since this is your attitude and you have not kept my covenant and my decrees, which I commanded you, I will most certainly tear the kingdom away from you and give it to one of your subordinates'" (1 Kings 11:11 NIV).

Because of his disobedience, Solomon missed God's best for him, his family, and the Israelites.

NEBUCHADNEZZAR'S DISOBEDIENCE IN THE FACE OF CLEAR WARNING

Nebuchadnezzar's conversion to become a worshipper of Yahweh is an amazing story. God put Daniel by his side to interpret his dreams and model a life lived in reverence to God. Nebuchadnezzar had several confrontations with Yahweh and His power, including the dream of the statue with the head of gold (Dan. 2) and the miraculous delivery of Shadrach, Meshach, and Abednego from the fiery furnace.

While these encounters caused him to offer respect and praise of Yahweh, he didn't yet worship Him as the one sovereign God, so God brought another dream to him (Dan. 4).

He saw a magnificent tree, which provided shelter for all the birds, food, and shade for the beasts below. Then a "holy one" from heaven came and ordered the tree to be cut down, its branches stripped. "But let the stump and its roots, bound with iron and bronze, remain in the ground, in the grass of the field. Let him be drenched with the dew of heaven, and let him live with the animals among the plants of the earth. Let his mind be changed from that of a man and let him be given the mind of an animal, till seven times pass by for him" (Dan. 4:15–16 NIV).

Nebuchadnezzar sent for Daniel, who because of his love and respect for the king painfully relayed the warning to Nebuchadnezzar that though he was powerful and successful as a ruler, unless he acknowledged Yahweh as God, he would be cut down and roam the fields like an animal for seven years. Daniel ended with this plea: "Therefore, O king, be pleased to accept my advice: Renounce your sins by doing what is right, and your wickedness by being kind to the oppressed. It may be that then your prosperity will continue" (Dan. 4:27 NIV).

One year went by, and the king didn't repent. Our God is a patient God, but there is a limit to His patience. After a year of no repentance, the king was on his roof, admiring his kingdom and accomplishments. "He said, 'Is not this the great Babylon I have built as the royal residence, by my mighty power and for the glory of my majesty?'" (Dan. 4:30 NIV).

Before he could utter another word, God struck him, as the dream had warned, and the king became like an animal in the fields for the next seven years.

Those were painful circumstances that could have been avoided. We aren't told about all the unintended consequences to his family and the kingdom because of his disobedience, but he clearly missed God's best for him through disobedience.

The great ending to this story is that we learn about this dream and the seven-year banishment in the context of a narrative, which Nebuchadnezzar himself penned (Dan. 4). It concludes like this: "Now I, Nebuchadnezzar, praise and exalt and glorify the King of heaven, because everything he does is right and all his ways are just. And those who walk in pride he is able to humble" (Dan. 4:37 NIV).

Nebuchadnezzar bent his knee to Yahweh because of God's love, patience, and discipline in his life; but he brought on himself consequences he didn't have to bear. We miss God's best through disobedience.

THE RICH YOUNG RULER'S DISOBEDIENCE

What is the name of the rich young ruler? His story is found in Matthew 19:16; Mark 10:17; and Luke 18:18. But we don't know his name.

After a brief conversation, in which the rich young ruler asserted to Jesus that he had led a "good" life by keeping the commandments, Jesus showed him that while he had been a student of the law and kept its precepts, he didn't have a love for God. Jesus made him an incredible offer. "When Jesus heard this, he said to him, 'You still lack one thing. Sell everything you have and give to the poor, and you will have treasure in heaven. Then come, follow me'" (Luke 18:22 NIV).

Jesus gave this man an opportunity to become one of His disciples, an apostle. How awesome! Who wouldn't have jumped at such an opportunity? We would certainly have known his name if he'd accepted Jesus's offer. He may have even become one of the Gospel writers. Instead, the condition Jesus put on becoming a disciple was too costly for him. He loved his wealth more than his relationship with God, and his name is lost to us; perhaps even his soul was lost as well.

He was offered everything eternal, but he chose to keep what was temporal. In his decision, he missed out on God's best for him.

Here are some additional thoughts: "For we are God's workmanship, created in Christ Jesus to do good works, which God prepared in advance for us to do" (Eph. 2:10 NIV). If we remain focused on our relationship with Jesus and do the work He prepared in advance for us to do, we can experience the richest life possible, both on earth and in heaven.

However, we will all be disobedient at some point in our lives, perhaps many times; and each time we will incur consequences God never intended us to bear. We will miss out on God's best for us through disobedience.

I have made mistakes, been willfully disobedient in my life, and suffered consequences that affected me and all those within my sphere of influence and perhaps even beyond. Truthfully, some of those mistakes may have disqualified me from serving in some kingdom roles. Reuben, Simeon, and Levi were disqualified from receiving the birthright blessing (and consequently being in the lineage of Christ) because of their disobedience.

I take comfort, however, in the way God restored David. Despite suffering terrible consequences for his disobedience, God described him centuries later as "My servant David" (Ezk 34:23 NIV).

Forgiveness and reconciliation with God are possible regardless of the offense, but the key that gives us access to that gift is repentance. This isn't just a contrite attitude for having been caught or having to suffer consequences but an attitude of contempt for the disobedient deed and the suffering it has caused and a passionate desire to never commit the despicable act again.

I want God's best for me and all those whose lives I impact. Lord, help me to despise anything that competes with my love for You.

MEGATHEME 5:

THROUGH OUR OBEDIENCE, MANY ARE BLESSED, AND THROUGH OUR DISOBEDIENCE, MANY SUFFER; THERE ARE NO OTHER OUTCOMES

I have heard many people say, "Oh, this sin is between me and God. It concerns no one else." My challenge to them is, "Name a 'private' sin—that is, a sin that only affects you!" Let me give you just one example of a "private" sin that has been offered in response to this question: pornography.

Several young men, even married ones, told me that looking at pornography affected them and no one else. Here was my response: "Besides the destructive addiction you are inviting into your life; besides the fact that you are encouraging—even supporting—a demonic industry with every 'view' or 'rental;' besides the fact that you are subconsciously setting expectations for your wife or future wife that she can never meet. Then there is the fact that you are filling your mind with images that are displeasing to God, and it will take you years, if ever, to erase them; besides all this, your relationship with God is broken. Through your disobedience, everyone in your sphere of influence is being denied the godly man you have the potential to be, a man who could be their encouragement and example. Instead, you present them with a man who is spiritually crippled."

Every sin, no matter where or how the act or thought is actualized, breaks our fellowship with God and denies us the spiritual authority and power He is willing to give us. All those in our sphere of influence and beyond suffer for our sin because we are no longer the man or woman of spiritual power and authority God intended us to be for them.

Look at this example: "For just as through the disobedience of the one man the many were made sinners, so also through the obedience of the one man the many will be made righteous" (Rom. 5:19 NIV).

We are all born spiritually dead because of the sin of one man—Adam. And there are many other examples of this megatheme in scripture. Just look at the examples from the previous section.

1. Abraham's lack of patience for Sarah to produce an heir
2. The disobedience of Jacob's oldest three sons: Reuben, Levi, and Simeon
3. The disobedience of Moses
4. Israel's disobedience in the desert
5. Saul's disobedience at Gilgal
6. David's disobedience with Uriah and Bathsheba
7. Solomon's disobedience regarding foreign wives
8. Nebuchadnezzar's disobedience in the face of clear warning
9. The rich young ruler's disobedience

Millions have suffered, even to this day, because of the individual disobedience and failures above. Sin always affects more than just you.

God didn't give us the Ten Commandments and the other "don'ts" of scripture to keep us from having fun. He gave us the commands so we might enjoy life, both in the present and in the eternal, to the fullest extent possible and not live with consequences He never intended us and others to bear.

How many families have you seen ruined, lives scarred permanently, because one man or woman disobeyed God's moral law? You know this megatheme to be existentially true; that is, life experience bears out the truth of this statement.

But just as disobedience brings pain and suffering to many through the sins of one person, the obedience of one person can bring blessing to many. Here are some examples:

Abraham obeyed God and attempted to offer his son Isaac as a sacrifice to God. God's response was the following: "The angel of the Lord called to Abraham from heaven a second time and said, 'I swear by myself, declares the Lord, that because you have done this and have not withheld your son, your only son, I will surely bless you and make your descendants as numerous as the stars in the sky and as the sand on the seashore. Your descendants will take possession of the cities of their enemies, and through your offspring all nations on earth will be blessed, because you have obeyed me'" (Gen. 22:15–18 NIV). An entire nation was born and given a promise that extends to this day.

Gideon faced a formidable enemy. He answered God's call to raise an army and then prune his army down to three hundred hand-selected men. Against overwhelming odds, he entered the battle against the Midianites. "Thus Midian was subdued before the Israelites and did not raise its head again. During Gideon's lifetime, the land enjoyed peace forty years" (Judg. 8:28 NIV). Many were blessed for forty years or more because of Gideon's obedience.

Esther risked her life to go before King Xerxes and plead for the life of her people. As a result, the evil Haman was executed, her uncle Mordecai was promoted to "second in rank to King Xerxes" (Est. 10:3), and the Jews were spared the executions Haman had plotted.

Given a second chance, Jonah obeyed God and went to Nineveh to warn of God's judgment and offer of escape through repentance. When the king of Nineveh heard Jonah's words, he responded with obedience: "When the news reached the king of Nineveh, he rose from his throne, took off his royal robes, covered himself with sackcloth and sat down in the dust" (Jon. 3:6 NIV).

And God responded: "When God saw what they did and how they turned from their evil ways, he had compassion and did not bring upon them the destruction he had threatened" (Jon. 3:10 NIV).

Thousands, if not millions, of lives were spared because of the obedience of Jonah and the king's obedient response. Philip went to

Samaria to preach the gospel, and many responded. "But when they believed Philip as he preached the good news of the kingdom of God and the name of Jesus Christ, they were baptized, both men and women" (Acts 8:12 NIV).

We also have every reason to believe the Ethiopian heard the gospel because of Philip's obedience. "Now an angel of the Lord said to Philip, 'Go south to the road—the desert road—that goes down from Jerusalem to Gaza.' So he started out, and on his way he met an Ethiopian eunuch, an important official in charge of all the treasury of Candace, queen of the Ethiopians. This man had gone to Jerusalem to worship" (Acts 8:26–27 NIV).

The eunuch was baptized and no doubt returned to Ethiopia with the good news.

What about now? Does God still bless many through the obedience of one? I know a man who, while he was living in disobedience to God, experienced confrontation from God for his sin. That man repented and became a passionate follower of Jesus. Today, he is surrounded by a godly family, has been entrusted with spiritual authority, and is a mentor to many. I have heard some refer to him as "a General in the Kingdom of God."

If this man had persisted in disobedience after receiving God's rebuke, I believe his story would have had a much different ending; many would have suffered. But through his obedience, many have been blessed, both now and for eternity to come.

By our disobedience, many suffer; by our obedience, many are blessed. There are no other outcomes.

MEGATHEME 6:

SIN'S NATURE IS PROGRESSIVE: WE TOLERATE IT IN OUR LIVES (1 KINGS 11:1–2), WE BEGIN TO PARTICIPATE IN IT (11:3–6), AND WE LIVE IT BOLDLY AND PUBLICLY (11:7–8)

One of the most disappointing characters in all scripture for me is Solomon. Earlier we listed the progression of Solomon's disobedience, from marrying many foreign wives against God's command to setting up altars for them to worship their gods and to actually worshipping their gods himself.

What an amazing inheritance he was given: a godly father (the most admired king of Israel to this day), great wealth, and—at his request—wisdom from God. He became one of the wisest men in the world.

The queen of Sheba met Solomon and engaged him in conversation. She said this afterward: "How happy your men must be! How happy your officials, who continually stand before you and hear your wisdom! Praise be to the Lord your God, who has delighted in you and placed you on the throne of Israel. Because of the Lord's eternal love for Israel, he has made you king, to maintain justice and righteousness" (1 Kings 10:8–9 NIV).

How does his life end after he built altars to Molech and other gods? For this disobedience, God divided the kingdom of Israel into northern and southern parts, with Solomon's son, Rehoboam, retaining only two of the twelve tribes. This began the decline of Israel, with many suffering because of Solomon's disobedience.

I'm sure that if you had told Solomon early in his reign that he would eventually sacrifice to foreign gods, he would have denied this statement as a preposterous suggestion. I know few people today who think their disobedience—their sin—will ever progress to divorce, rape, murder, prison, or addiction. Temptation just doesn't work that way. Few people would jump at the offer to spend ten or more years in prison, but many will watch the first pornographic film, exchange an improper e-mail with a coworker, or sample an addictive substance "just this once." This is the nature of temptation.

James 1:14–15 (NIV) says, "But each one is tempted when, by his own evil desire, he is dragged away and enticed. Then, after desire has conceived, it gives birth to sin; and sin, when it is full-grown, gives birth to death." Listen to what Thomas a' Kempis said about temptation in *Imitation of Christ*. "Yet we must be watchful, especially in the beginning of temptation, for the enemy is more easily overcome in the beginning if he is not allowed to enter the door of our hearts, but is resisted outside the gate, at his first knock. When he is not resisted, little by little, he gets complete entrance" (book one, 13:5e).

Scripture warns us, "Therefore each of you must put off falsehood and speak truthfully to his neighbor, for we are all members of one body. 'In your anger do not sin.' Do not let the sun go down while you are still angry, and do not give the devil a foothold" (Eph. 4:25–27 NIV).

"Do not give the devil a foothold!" Let me just say that when we willfully disobey God and engage in behavior we know God has condemned, we open our souls to the demons of hell. We invite the demonic host to reside in our inner being, that place where only God should reign.

I'm not talking about demonic possession here, though that's possible with unbelievers. I'm suggesting that we quench the gentle voice and promptings of the Spirit; we harden our hearts such that the demonic influence in our lives becomes the dominant one. The enemy reigns in our decision-making instead of Jesus.

This is why the temptation must be resisted while it is outside the gate. And how do we do this? Second Corinthians 10:4–5 (NIV) says, "The weapons we fight with are not the weapons of the world. On the contrary, they have divine power to demolish strongholds. We demolish arguments and every pretension that sets itself up against the knowledge of God, and we take captive every thought to make it obedient to Christ."

What does it mean to "take captive every thought to make it obedient to Christ"?

When we pick up the smartphone late at night and are tempted to search on an adult video site, we must drop to our knees and say, "Lord, I do not want to break fellowship with You. Help me, encourage me, deliver me!" Then we must turn to our Bible app and read scripture instead. This is how Jesus resisted Satan's temptations—with the word—which He had stored in His mind so He could recall it whenever and wherever He needed it.

When we are invited to participate in an activity we know is displeasing to God, we must stop, close our eyes, and say, "Lord, I do not want to lose the spiritual authority that You are willing to give me as an obedient servant, ambassador, and adopted son or daughter!" Then we say no and turn our focus to thoughts of our position in Christ as His representatives to all those in our sphere of influence.

When we see a beautiful person passing our field of view, when the look becomes a gaze and the imagination begins to darken our thoughts, we should redirect our focus and even close our eyes and say, "Lord, I do not want to bring unintended consequences on anyone in my sphere of influence. I want to be an agent for good, not evil; for blessing, not destruction." Then we should turn our focus to "whatever is true, whatever is noble, whatever is right, whatever is pure, whatever is lovely, whatever is admirable—anything that is excellent or praiseworthy—think about such things" (Phil. 4:8).

Don't try to fight temptation alone. Find a small group where you can confess your sins one to another and hold each other accountable for the weaknesses you have; you will all have one or more vulnerable spots in your "armor." Give each of the people in your small group the permission to ask you anytime, "How are you doing with that?" It's a powerful thing to know that if you succumb to a temptation, you will have to admit it or lie when your friends ask you about it. Both are painful moments, and the lie option only postpones the pain while accumulating more consequences.

Finally, a word here on the value of scripture memorization in defeating temptation: "taking every thought captive." I heard someone say once, "Even God cannot help you recall what you don't know!" Yes, God can give us revelation, but that isn't recall. You can recall only what you have previously learned and stored away.

When we take the time to memorize scripture, not only do we store up weapons to use in any spiritual battle or temptation we might face, but we also increase our usefulness to Jesus. How? When you know a scripture someone in your sphere of influence needs to hear because of his or her circumstances and struggles, Jesus can use you in your encounter with that person to bring this to your mind to share with him or her. If you didn't know that passage, He would have to use another (or use someone else who did know the proper passage). I am amazed by how often I have found a passage to be helpful to a friend shortly after I took the time to memorize it.

I don't want to lose the spiritual power and authority the Lord Jesus is willing to entrust to me. I don't want to lose the opportunity to be His agent for grace and blessing to all those in my sphere of influence. I want Jesus to point out anything to me that could hinder our relationship so I might come to recognize it and despise it.

Sin's nature is progressive; stop it at the gate.

THE GOSPEL IS GOOD NEWS

The gospel stands apart from all other world religions because it is, first and foremost, not a religion. This chapter offers several megathemes that speak to the uniqueness of the gospel and how it is truly good news to all who embrace it.

MEGATHEME 7:

OTHER WORLD RELIGIONS SAY, "DO AND YOU WILL BE ACCEPTED." THE GOSPEL SAYS, "YOU ARE ACCEPTED; THEREFORE DO"

> But because of his great love for us, God, who is rich in mercy, made us alive with Christ even when we were dead in transgressions—it is by grace you have been saved. And God raised us up with Christ and seated us with him in the heavenly realms in Christ Jesus, in order that in the coming ages he might show the incomparable riches of his grace, expressed in his kindness to us in Christ Jesus. For it is by grace you have been saved, through faith—and this not from yourselves, it is the gift of God—not by works, so that no one can boast. (Eph. 2:4–9 NIV)

This is the gospel, the "good news," every follower of Jesus should live out. I owe much of the content of this section to the teachings and writings of Tim Keller (founding pastor of Redeemer Presbyterian Church in New York City), who has affected my understanding of, and appreciation for, the gospel immensely.

I want to offer three truths to you in this section:

- The gospel is unique among all other world religions.
- The gospel is not a religion.
- The gospel is good news.

If someone asked you why you were a follower of Jesus, how would you answer the question? When I ask this question of people who profess Christianity as their faith, over half give me an answer that can be paraphrased as "because I was raised in a Christian home" or "because my mother and father were Christian." Let me say that there couldn't be a poorer response to this question than those answers.

Why are you a follower of Jesus? If you have never really done the critical thinking required to articulate why you believe Jesus is worthy of worship and obedience, you cannot engage in a more important use of your time and resources. If you aren't sure which—if any—world religion is true, you cannot engage in a more valuable use of your resources than to do a comparative analysis of them to see which is the truest (that is, which of them best explains life and the world as you see and experience them?).

Some have said, "Aren't all religions basically the same, promoting the Golden Rule and love for one another?" Actually, they aren't. They may have some moral percepts in common, but their views and descriptions of things such as God, man, sin, salvation, heaven, hell, and so forth are not only widely divergent but in most cases mutually exclusive. Listen to what Stephen Prothro, professor of religion at Boston University (an agnostic), says in his book *God Is Not One!*

> To claim that all religions are the same is to deny the differences among a Buddhist who believes in no god, a Jew who believes in one God, and a Hindu who believes in many gods.
>
> This is a lovely sentiment, but it is dangerous, disrespectful, and untrue.
>
> The world's religious rivals do converge when it comes to ethics, but they diverge sharply on doctrine, ritual, mythology, experience, and law.
>
> Faith in the unity of religions is just that—faith (perhaps even a kind of fundamentalism). And the leap that gets us there is an act of the hyperactive imagination.

So how would one begin a critical review of the world's religions if one were in search of the truth?

Suppose there was one true religion, and you wanted to obscure its truth. How might you do so? One way would be to create many alternative but false variations. Then how could anyone recognize the truth among so many imposters?

This appears to be what has happened. There are thousands of religions in the world, and I would expect the imposters to have many common traits, since they are all intended to misrepresent the truth, and the truth would stand out as unique among all the others. In other words, the impostors would have more in common with each other than they would with the one true alternative. And that is exactly what we find in the gospel.

A. THE GOSPEL IS UNIQUE AMONG ALL OTHER WORLD RELIGIONS

It was pointed out to me years back that there is a major distinguishing characteristic of the gospel from all competing alternatives. In all world religions, there is a message and a messenger; there is a truth to be told and a messenger that points to the truth. Look closely at the chart below, which is only a sampling of some of the major world religions:

Religion	Messenger	Message
Buddhism	Buddha	Vedas
Hinduism	Multiple	Pali Canon
Islam	Mohammed	Koran
Mormonism	Joseph Smith	Book of Mormon
Jehovah Witness	Charles Russell	Zion's Watchtower
Christian Science	Mary Baker Eddy	Science & Health
Scientology	L. Ron Hubbard	Dianetics
Judaism	Moses, prophets	OT and Talmud
Christianity	The Bible	Jesus

Notice that for every religion except Christianity, the message is a book, and the messenger is a person. Some person points to a book as the truth that needs to be learned and followed. But in Christianity, the situation is reversed. The message is a person (Jesus), and the messenger is a book (the Bible), which points to the truth. A person to be studied and followed.

John 14:6 (NIV) says, "Jesus answered, 'I am the way and the truth and the life. No one comes to the Father except through me.'" Notice Jesus didn't say, "I point you to the way." He said, "I *am* the way" (emphasis added).

Luke 24:27 NIV) says, "And beginning with Moses and all the Prophets, he explained to them what was said in all the Scriptures concerning himself." On the road to Emmaus, Jesus explained to the two disciples with whom He was walking that the scriptures (Old Testament canon) pointed the way to Himself, the truth.

The founders of other major religions came as teachers (messengers), not as saviors (the message). This distinguishing characteristic of the gospel makes it worthy of investigation and critical study as perhaps the truth the enemy is trying to counterfeit with many false alternatives—alternatives that are more like each other than they are different.

Here is another major distinguishing characteristic of the gospel.

B. THE GOSPEL IS NOT A RELIGION

Christianity stands alone among the world religions as a covenant rather than a contract. What is the difference?

In a contract, one does something in return, for which the other party responds with services or rewards. In a covenant, the agreement is one sided; one party decides to provide services or rewards based on no merit on the part of the other party.

All other world religions are "contracts."

World Religions—We contribute to our salvation through our moral efforts.

The Gospel—We are saved not by our moral efforts but by Christ's righteousness, which is offered freely to us based on His merit (life, death, and resurrection), not ours.

World Religions—Do this, and you will find the divine.

The Gospel (Jesus)—"I am the Divine and come to you to do for you what you could not do for yourself."

World Religions—I do; therefore, God does.

The Gospel—God has done; therefore, I do.

The gospel is unique because it's not about finding your way to the divine through your effort; it is about being rescued by the Divine via His effort. Colossians 1:13–14 (NIV) says, "For he has rescued us from the dominion of darkness and brought us into the kingdom of the Son he loves, in whom we have redemption, the forgiveness of sins."

So Christianity (the gospel) isn't a religion because it stands apart from all other world religions as being unique in messenger versus message and covenant versus contract. It is more correct to say that the gospel is a relationship (in other words, it's about a Person to be followed) rather than a religion (a set of tenets to be followed).

And this further distinguishes the gospel as exceptionally good news.

C. THE GOSPEL IS GOOD NEWS

Here is a compare/contrast view of how the gospel (specifically, the person of Jesus) working within us has power to help us cope with life and death:

	Religion (See *)	Gospel
Strategy	Save myself.	Trust myself to Christ.
Goal	Accumulate merits.	Know God.
Description	Burden bearer	God lover
Motive for Obedience	Fear	Gratitude
Self-Regard	Superiority/Loathing	Humility/Deep confidence
Treatment of Others	Devalue	Love

Handling Adversity	Anger	Confidence/peace
View of Grace	I do not need it.	I desperately need it.
View of Sin	I'm always guilty	I am exonerated.
Condition	Weary	Grateful

* Note: This column doesn't suggest that every follower of a world religion other than the gospel has this attitude. We should judge a religion by its founder and his or her teachings, not by his or her followers (and that includes Christianity). Few people adhere to the tenets of their faith perfectly. This column captures the result of the teachings of religion or the gospel if one follows it as the messenger and message taught.

The gospel is unique among world religions because it's a covenant of grace, not a contract of moral effort. We don't need to wonder about our standing with God or compete with others to improve our standing.

Human beings have two needs (longings):

1. Every human being longs to feel okay (unconditionally accepted).
2. Every human being longs to escape shame and guilt for his or her sins.

Religion can't satisfy either longing. You can never do enough to feel okay or escape your guilt and shame. But the gospel can satisfy both. God loved you so much that He paid your ransom to free you from sin's bondage. You are more than okay; you are a child of the eternal, living God. Psalm 103:10–11 (NIV) says,

> He does not treat us as our sins deserve
> or repay us according to our iniquities.
> For as high as the heavens are above the earth,
> so great is his love for those who fear him.

What about your guilt and shame? The gospel isn't a pardon (which suspends your sentence while keeping your guilty status); it's exoneration (declaring you "not guilty"—you didn't do it; someone else has admitted to the crime and has taken the punishment for that crime). Psalm 103:12 (NIV) says,

> As far as the east is from the west,
> so far has he removed our transgressions from us.

The gospel isn't a religion; the gospel isn't practiced as a religion. The gospel is a relationship with the God who has rescued us. It's a covenant from Him to us, not a contract based on our performance. It is indeed good news.

MEGATHEME 8:

THERE ARE ONLY TWO RESPONSES TO GRACE: GRATITUDE OR CONTEMPT

If you have never read the French historical novel *Les Misérables* by Victor Hugo or seen one of the many films based on the book, you would do well to familiarize yourself with the story.

Two characters are shown grace: Jean Valjean and Inspector Javert. One changes his life and becomes a man of generosity and humility out of thanksgiving for the grace shown to him. The other, a strict legalist, cannot accept the grace shown to him. The grace confuses him profoundly, and ultimately, he escapes the tension by committing suicide.

The story shows the two possible responses to grace: gratitude or contempt. Those who know they need grace are grateful to find it; those who don't think they need it not only don't seek it but despise others who receive it.

Before we go any further, what is grace? I am not a Hebrew scholar, but I was recently introduced to the Hebrew word *hesed*, from which we translate words like *loving-kindness*, *mercy*, *loyalty*, and *grace*. I have been told that the best definition of the word is when one from whom I have no right to expect anything gives me everything. This will be our working definition of *grace*.

THE CONCEPT IN SCRIPTURE

Romans 2:4 (NIV) says, "Or do you show contempt for the riches of his kindness, tolerance and patience, not realizing that God's kindness leads you toward repentance?" I know people who are perplexed that God seems to treat the lost with kindness and patience. They ask, "Why do the wicked prosper?" But God says kindness (grace) is His primary approach to dealing with the lost. Jesus also affirmed this. Luke 4:22 (NIV) says, "All spoke well of him and were amazed at the gracious words that came from his lips."

The priests in the OT were given the role of intercessor for God's people, which was an act of grace on behalf of God. They were tempted to perform their duties with contempt. Leviticus 22:9 (NIV) says, "The priests are to keep my requirements so that they do not become guilty and die for treating them with contempt. I am the Lord, who makes them holy."

Isaiah said that when the wicked are offered grace, they go on "doing evil," showing contempt by their actions for the grace shown them.

> Though grace is shown to the wicked,
> they do not learn righteousness;
> even in a land of uprightness they go on doing evil
> and regard not the majesty of the Lord.
> (Isa. 26:10 NIV)

And after God performed amazing feats among the Israelites (grace), they still showed Him contempt. Numbers 14:11 (NIV) says, "The Lord said to Moses, 'How long will these people treat me with contempt? How long will they refuse to believe in me, in spite of all the miraculous signs I have performed among them?'"

Let's look at some individual responses to grace in scripture.

RESPONDING TO GRACE WITH GRATITUDE

Jacob

Jacob deceived his brother, Esau, and stole his birthright from him. He fled from his home out of fear of Esau. But God showed favor to Jacob through his father-in-law, Laban, and then through a direct encounter with God at Peniel (Gen. 32:22–32). The latter occurred the evening before he was to meet his brother, Esau, for the first time after they had separated. At the end of his encounter with God, he said, "I saw God face to face, and yet my life was spared" (Gen. 32:30 NIV).

As Jacob neared Esau, Jacob sent gifts ahead to show his brother the change in his heart. And when he met Esau, this is what happened. "'No, please!' said Jacob. 'If I have found favor in your eyes, accept this gift from me. For to see your face is like seeing the face of God, now that you have received me favorably. Please accept the present that was brought to you, for God has been gracious to me and I have all I need.' And because Jacob insisted, Esau accepted it" (Gen. 33:10–11 NIV).

God's favor and then Esau's double grace had the effect of humbling Jacob and cultivating a grateful attitude.

Joseph

Genesis 50:19–21 (NIV) says, "But Joseph said to them, 'Don't be afraid. Am I in the place of God? You intended to harm me, but God intended it for good to accomplish what is now being done, the saving of many lives. So then, don't be afraid. I will provide for you and your children.' And he reassured them and spoke kindly to them."

After Joseph's brothers sorely mistreated him, God showed him grace and made him prime minister of all Egypt. Joseph put his brothers' fears to rest after their father's, Jacob's, death with these words: "Don't be afraid. I will provide for you and your children." Joseph was a recipient of grace, showing grace in response.

Mephibosheth

Mephibosheth is one of my favorite grace stories in all scripture. He was the son of Jonathan, the grandson of Saul, and crippled due to a childhood injury. David inquired one day, "Is there anyone still left of the house of Saul to whom I can show kindness for Jonathan's sake?" (2 Sam. 9:1). When he was told about Mephibosheth, he had him brought to him and said this to him: "'Don't be afraid,' David said to him, 'for I will surely show you kindness for the sake of your father Jonathan. I will restore to you all the land that belonged to your grandfather Saul, and you will always eat at my table'" (2 Sam. 9:7 NIV).

From that day on, Mephibosheth ate at the king's table as though he were royalty. From one from whom he had no right to expect anything, he received everything.

PARABLE OF THE PRODIGAL SON, THE YOUNGER BROTHER

"So he got up and went to his father. But while he was still a long way off, his father saw him and was filled with compassion for him; he ran to his son, threw his arms around him and kissed him. The son said to him, 'Father, I have sinned against heaven and against you. I am no longer worthy to be called your son'" (Luke 15:20–21 NIV).

One of the most well-known Bible stories is a great example of this megatheme of scripture. The younger son, who had disrespected his father and squandered his inheritance, went home. Before he could say a word, his running father met him with a huge embrace and a kiss. His response? Gratitude.

SOME DIFFERENT RESPONSES TO GRACE: CONTEMPT

Nabal

While David was fleeing from Saul, he and his men fled to the desert of Moan. There was a prominent, wealthy man there named

Nabal. David and his men had voluntarily provided protection for Nabal's shepherds and his flocks, and when time to shear the sheep arrived, David sent messengers to ask Nabal for any provisions he could spare for him and his men. Here is Nabal's response:

"Nabal answered David's servants, 'Who is this David? Who is this son of Jesse? Many servants are breaking away from their masters these days. Why should I take my bread and water, and the meat I have slaughtered for my shearers, and give it to men coming from who knows where?'" (1 Sam. 25:10–11 NIV).

Nabal didn't think he needed David's protection, even though his own men disagreed (1 Sam. 25:14–16). Nabal's response is typical of those who receive grace they don't believe they need; they despise and reject it. Nabal's contempt for David and his gesture of grace cost him his life.

Absalom

Here is another tragic story from scripture. Absalom's half-brother Amnon raped his sister, Tamar. David didn't punish Amnon, and eventually Absalom took out his vengeance on Amnon and killed him. Absalom, fearing the wrath of David, fled Jerusalem.

Now these aren't David's finest moments, but he eventually invited Absalom back to Jerusalem with no threat of revenge. He took another two years before inviting him into his presence. Before we judge David too harshly, we need to remember he was the king. His son had been murdered at the hands of Absalom, and he had no obligation to offer Absalom grace. He had every right to have him killed, but he did ask to see Absalom. "Then the king summoned Absalom, and he came in and bowed down with his face to the ground before the king. And the king kissed Absalom" (2 Sam. 14:33 NIV).

What was Absalom's response after having been shown forgiveness and grace?

"Then Absalom sent secret messengers throughout the tribes of Israel to say, 'As soon as you hear the sound of the trumpets, then say, "Absalom is king in Hebron"'" (2 Sam. 15:10 NIV).

He organized an effort to usurp the throne from David and eventually lost his life. There is a pattern emerging here: those who don't think they need grace despise it (show contempt for it) when offered, and this attitude costs them their lives.

The Prodigal Son's Older Brother

The younger son was offered grace and embraced it with gratitude. The older son had been offered grace also. Luke 15:31 (NIV) says, "'My son,' the father said, 'you are always with me, and everything I have is yours.'"

He saw his inheritance as a right, an entitlement, but it wasn't. His father pointed out that he had been graciously offered two things (note the order).

1. To be with the father
2. To have everything the father owned

Luke 15:29–30 (NIV) says, "But he answered his father, 'Look! All these years I've been slaving for you and never disobeyed your orders. Yet you never gave me even a young goat so I could celebrate with my friends. But when this son of yours who has squandered your property with prostitutes comes home, you kill the fattened calf for him!'"

He didn't value the presence of the father, only his stuff; and because he believed the stuff was his by birth, he couldn't see the grace in the father's provision for him. Thus, he treated the father and his bother with contempt. Those who don't think they need grace despise it when it's offered to them, and they resent those who do receive it.

Judas

Another tragedy of scripture is the result of grace rejected.

Mark 6:7–12 (NIV) says, "Calling the Twelve to him, he sent them out two by two and gave them authority over evil spirits. These were his instructions: 'Take nothing for the journey except a staff—no bread, no bag, no money in your belts. Wear sandals but not an extra tunic. Whenever you enter a house, stay there until you leave that town. And if any place will not welcome you or listen to you, shake the dust off your feet when you leave, as a testimony against them.' They went out and preached that people should repent."

Judas is among the twelve here who were given power to preach the gospel and confront and command demons. Judas was given a privileged position to be among the twelve apostles who were destined to sit on a throne and judge Israel.

Matthew 19:28 (NIV) says, "Jesus said to them, 'I tell you the truth, at the renewal of all things, when the Son of Man sits on his glorious throne, you who have followed me will also sit on twelve thrones, judging the twelve tribes of Israel.'"

But what was his response to this amazing offer?

"Then one of the Twelve—the one called Judas Iscariot—went to the chief priests and asked, 'What are you willing to give me if I hand him over to you?' So they counted out for him thirty silver coins. From then on Judas watched for an opportunity to hand him over" (Matt. 26:14–16 NIV).

His is the same contemptuous response and the same result, death. What is it about grace that leads us to make one of two polar-opposite responses?

GRACE COVERS THE PERCEIVED GAP BETWEEN OUR "GOODNESS" AND GOD'S HOLINESS

I believe the reason some people reject and resent grace is that they have a perception of their own goodness that is overstated and a perception of God's holiness and righteousness that is understated. That is, they think highly of themselves and poorly of God. Thinking themselves to be as good or better than most, and thinking God to be tolerant and accommodating of any sin, especially theirs, they are led to have a low regard for grace.

You see, grace is what bridges the gap between our "goodness" and God's holiness. How big is this gap in reality? The Bible says no one is good but God alone.

> The Lord looks down from heaven
> on the sons of men
> to see if there are any who understand,
> any who seek God.
> All have turned aside,
> they have together become corrupt;
> there is no one who does good,
> not even one.
> (Ps. 14:2–3 NIV)

> As Jesus started on his way, a man ran up to him and fell on his knees before him. "Good teacher," he asked, "what must I do to inherit eternal life?" "Why do you call me good?" Jesus answered. "No one is good— except God alone." (Mark 10:17–18 NIV)

If none are good, only God, then the gap is infinite. I need grace. I have no way of making up for bad things done in the past, because any good I would do for extra credit is good a "good man" would be doing anyway. I cannot bridge the gap between myself and God.

GRACE CAN BE APPRECIATED ONLY BY THOSE WHO KNOW THEY NEED IT

Luke 18:11–12 (NIV) says, "The Pharisee stood up and prayed about himself: 'God, I thank you that I am not like other men— robbers, evildoers, adulterers—or even like this tax collector. I fast twice a week and give a tenth of all I get.'"

If I believe I'm not too far from God in my own goodness or see my sins as very small compared to everyone else's, not only will I not believe I need grace, but I will resent the fact that other people receive it. From my perspective, they get to have their fun (while I sit here and slave for God), and we both get the same reward—forgiveness and eternal life.

This was the attitude of the older brother in the parable about the prodigal son.

CONTEMPT IS THE ATTITUDE OF GOD'S ENEMIES

My attitude toward grace, when I don't believe I need it, is to loathe it, to have contempt for it, because it allows those worse than I am to receive the same gift from God—eternal life.

This is a dangerous attitude, contempt for God, and His offer of grace to us. Scripture is clear that contempt is the attitude God's enemies have toward Him.

> Not one of them will ever see the land I promised on oath to their forefathers. No one who has treated me with contempt will ever see it. (Num. 14:23 NIV)

> Multitudes who sleep in the dust of the earth will awake: some to everlasting life, others to shame and everlasting contempt. (Dan. 12:2 NIV)

> "But he will reply, 'I don't know you or where you come from. Away from me, all you evildoers!' There will be weeping there, and gnashing of teeth, when you see Abraham, Isaac and Jacob and all the prophets in the kingdom of God, but you yourselves thrown out." (Luke 13:27–28 NIV)

What is this "gnashing of teeth"? We see this in scripture when an injured person was taking out his or her vengeance on the person who caused his or her injury.

> Like the ungodly they maliciously mocked;
> they gnashed their teeth at me.
> (Ps. 35:16 NIV)

When they heard this, they were furious and gnashed their teeth at him. (Acts 7:54 NIV)

We have gestures in our culture that signify contempt for a person; as did the Israelites, and theirs was to gnash their teeth at someone as if to say, "I would chew you up and spit you out." This is the attitude people in hell will have toward God. This is why it's a dangerous attitude for anyone to have toward God at any time.

There are only two responses to God's offer of grace to us: gratitude and contempt. If your response leans toward the latter, you need to revisit your understanding of God's holiness and your goodness; the gap for you is too small.

MEGATHEME 9:

THERE IS NO FORGIVENESS (GRACE) WITHOUT REPENTANCE

Is this the teaching of scripture? Why is it important? Can't God just forgive us without any strings attached? Let's examine scripture first.

> The Lord is not slow in keeping his promise, as some understand slowness. He is patient with you, not wanting anyone to perish, but everyone to come to repentance. (2 Peter 3:9 NIV)

> Therefore let us leave the elementary teachings about Christ and go on to maturity, not laying again the foundation of repentance from acts that lead to death, and of faith in God. (Heb. 6:1 NIV)

> Godly sorrow brings repentance that leads to salvation and leaves no regret, but worldly sorrow brings death. (2 Cor. 7:10 NIV)

I have declared to both Jews and Greeks that they must turn to God in repentance and have faith in our Lord Jesus. (Acts 20:21 NIV)

The Spirit and the bride say, "Come!" And let him who hears say, "Come!" Whoever is thirsty, let him come; and whoever wishes, let him take the free gift of the water of life. (Rev. 22:17 NIV)

For it is by grace you have been saved, through faith—and this not from yourselves, it is the gift of God—not by works, so that no one can boast. (Eph. 2:8–9 NIV)

Jesus answered her, "If you knew the gift of God and who it is that asks you for a drink, you would have asked him and he would have given you living water." (John 4:10 NIV)

Scripture is clear. Salvation is the free gift of God, but it can be received only through a repentant faith. There is no forgiveness without repentance. Some key examples from scripture are the following:

Joseph, while fostering a forgiving heart toward his brothers, withheld pronouncing his forgiveness until they had shown their remorse and admitted their guilt (Gen 42:21–23; 45).

Jesus made it clear that repentance precedes forgiveness.

"The time has come," he said. "The kingdom of God is near. Repent and believe the good news!" (Mark 1:15 NIV)

I tell you, no! But unless you repent, you too will all perish. (Luke 13:3 NIV)

> Repent, then, and turn to God, so that your sins may
> be wiped out, that times of refreshing may come from
> the Lord. (Acts 3:19 NIV)

Repentance is a recognition that our sins are an affront to God and that they cost God greatly to be in a position to forgive our sins. It is a reversal, a turning from an attitude of rebellion and/or indifference to God to one of submission and obedience to God.

God is in a position to forgive our sins because of the life/death/resurrection of Christ, and He applies the righteousness of His Son in place of our sinfulness when we repent. It is an act of grace when One from whom I have no right to expect anything gives me everything.

Repentance doesn't earn salvation or forgiveness; it is the key that unlocks the riches of God's provision for us, which are there only because of His grace toward us.

God has always provided escape from coming doom for His people, but there was always a condition—one must accept His provision.

- The ark would save you from the flood, but you had to enter it.
- The angels would save you from destruction at Sodom and Gomorrah, but you had to go with them.
- The blood of a lamb on your doorpost would save you from the death angel, but you had to apply the blood.
- The manna would save you from starvation, but you had to go collect it.
- The serpent on the stick would save you from a snakebite, but you had to look at it.
- Christ offers forgiveness, atonement, or righteousness to save you from spiritual death, but you have to receive it through repentance, turning from an attitude of rebellion to obedience.

All the "escapes" above are offered because of the grace of God toward His people; none of us deserve it.

WHY CAN'T GOD JUST FORGIVE US ALL?

We have discussed two questions. Why couldn't God just forgive us all? Why did Jesus have to die? And we concluded with this: Jesus had to die so God could show men mercy, even grace, and still be just.

Now that Jesus has died for our sins, the question reemerges. Since God is now in a position to forgive my sins, why can't God just forgive us all? What the question asserts is this: If the gift of God is free, why can't He just give it to me without me having to repent?

We just discussed that there are only two responses to grace: gratitude or contempt. Consider taking a gift. Even if you say, "Thank you" and "Go away," wanting no other communication or contact with the gift giver is a form of contempt. Our actions say, "I want the gift, but I want nothing to do with the gift giver."

When anyone is offered a gift, he or she must choose to accept or reject it based on the terms of the gift giver. No gift giver will force you to accept a gift if you choose not to. God won't force you to accept His gift either. You must choose to do so freely, and the terms of His release of the gift to you is repentance. Why?

Christ didn't die just to save us from hell—separation from God; Christ died so we might have fellowship with God and become the sons and daughters of God we were intended to be. Romans 8:29 (NIV) says, "For those God foreknew he also predestined to be conformed to the likeness of his Son, that he might be the firstborn among many brothers."

God's design isn't to take us all to heaven so we can have a good time after death. If that were the case, then the question "Why not just forgive us all?" would be relevant. God's desire is that we would become like His Son, being obedient in every way and trusting completely in the goodness and loving kindness of the Father, and spend an eternity in fellowship with Him, His Son, the Holy Spirit, the angels, and one another. Giving us eternal life without an expressed desire on our part to be conformed to the image of Christ is inconsistent with God's intent for us.

Can I also add something? Having people in heaven with God

who don't want to be with God would ruin heaven for the rest of those who *do* want the joy of eternal fellowship with God. That would make heaven a continuation of earth, not heaven.

No one who truly wants to be "with God" has reluctance to repent of his or her ungodly ways, accepts the forgiveness offered through Jesus's sacrifice, and desires to be conformed to the ways of Christ. The requirement that repentance be required for forgiveness is consistent with God's goals for us.

Repentance is the response of gratitude. Any other response is utilitarian—wanting the things of God but not wanting God Himself, which is a response of contempt, the response of the enemies of God.

BUT ISN'T REPENTANCE A WORK?

You may say, "But our salvation is by faith alone, not works, so that no one may boast (Eph. 2:8); aren't you making repentance a work?" It is true that salvation is by faith alone; but if faith is merely the belief in the existence of God, Christ, and His offer of salvation, then it is something Satan and the demons demonstrate. Therefore, it cannot be saving faith (James 2:19).

Repentance isn't a work. It's not faith plus repentance that saves but rather a repentant faith. Repentance reveals the nature of the faith we have in God and Christ—that He and He alone is able to save, that we are willing to trust Him with our lives and submit to His authority, and that we want to become sons and daughters who please Him and fulfill the purpose for which we were created.

Repentance isn't a work that earns us the gift of forgiveness; it is the "how" of receiving the gift freely offered. Extending my hands to receive a gift doesn't earn the gift; the action just accepts it. A repentant faith is the way to extend our hands to accept God's free gift.

What about "Father forgive them, for they know not what they do"? Isn't this forgiveness without repentance?

This is a much-debated passage. There is even doubt as to whether this passage was in the original manuscripts, which is noted in most Bible translations. For this reason, it wouldn't be wise to build one's theology on a statement Jesus may not have made.

However, I believe it's likely Jesus did say this given the fact that Stephen, when he was being stoned, said almost the same thing of his murderers. "Lord, do not hold this sin against them!" (Acts 7:60). Stephen was probably modeling something he had heard or seen in Christ.

Assuming Jesus said this, was He asking the Father to forgive someone without repentance? Was Jesus basically saying, "Father, why can't You just forgive them (without repentance)?"

Jesus could have forgiven them, but He didn't. Why? He had demonstrated earlier that He had the power and authority to do so (Mark 2:10–11). He was willing to forgive. Both He and Stephen demonstrate this with their words. But it wasn't the time to pronounce the forgiveness. Why? Those who needed forgiveness hadn't yet demonstrated repentance, so pronouncement of forgiveness would have been premature. (Remember that Joseph did this with his brothers.) Jesus and Stephen deferred to another to pronounce the forgiveness after repentance was completed.

By deferring to the Father (in Jesus's case) and to Jesus (in Stephen's case), both were saying, "I am willing to forgive my offender; please forgive them according to Your will and purposes." They demonstrated hearts prepared to forgive, but the pronouncement of forgiveness was to come after repentance. These are great examples of putting "Love your enemies" into practice.

In both cases, the Father will forgive the offenders according to His plan for forgiveness, which occurs after repentance. I don't see a conflict with this passage if Jesus did, in fact, say this.

HOW DOES FORGIVENESS WORK THEN FOR ME?

The totality of scripture demands repentance before forgiveness. The objective is a restored relationship. An attitude of forgiveness can and should be fostered in the heart (as Joseph, Jesus, and Stephen did) toward forgiving the offender. But the pronouncement of forgiveness should be withheld until the offender repents (if that is possible).

Forgiveness has two objectives: absolve a debt and restore relationships.

When one person offends, injures, or causes loss to another, the injured person feels anger, hurt, and resentment. The relationship is broken, and two people are now in bondage.

1. The offender is in a position where he or she cannot or will not offer reparations—his or hers will become a bondage of guilt.
2. The offended is in bondage to revenge: feelings of anger and resentment toward the offender.

Forgiveness is God's way of freeing both the offender and the offended. It is meant to work this way:

1. The offended prepares his or her heart (as Jesus, Joseph, and Stephen did) to forgive the offender (absorb the debt if necessary) and desires that no further consequences on his or her part be placed on the offender. (This doesn't mean escaping the legal system, which is in place to ensure no one else is injured by an offender doing things that are illegal.) This frees the offended from his or her bondage to revenge.
2. The offender, when the person recognizes his or her guilt, goes to the offended and offers whatever reparations he or she can to remove or minimize the injury or loss (repentance).
3. The offended pronounces the forgiveness he or she has reserved for this moment. This frees the offender from his or her guilt and inability to repay the debt.
4. This restores the relationship. (It cannot be fully restored until all the steps above are completed.)

The relationship is restored because the offended is given the satisfaction that the offender, while he or she may not understand the depth of the hurt, pain, or loss he or she caused, did understand that he or she caused injury or loss. And it is only when offenders come to understand that they have caused this injury that forgiveness becomes something valued. In fact, if offenders don't believe they caused injury or loss, they will actually resent (show contempt for) the offer of forgiveness. (Remember, the response to grace by those who don't think they need it is contempt.)

God's forgiveness works the same way. We have offended God with our thoughts, words, deeds, and attitudes. God has prepared a way for us to receive forgiveness (through the work of His Son on the cross) and desires in His heart to forgive us. But our relationship is broken, and it can be repaired only when we come to acknowledge our debt to God, our injury to His holiness and His right to rule not only the universe but also our hearts and lives. This is repentance: acknowledging our wrongdoing before God, turning from that wrongdoing, and desiring to become the man or woman God gave us the potential to be. God responds with forgiveness, and our fellowship with God is restored.

Forgiveness is a gift from God at great cost to His Son; it isn't to be given to one who doesn't value or want it. True repentance comes from a heart that values God's gift, and it is this repentant faith that allows the offender to receive the gift of forgiveness.

There is no forgiveness without repentance.

MEGATHEME 10:

WE WILL BE JUDGED ACCORDING TO WHAT WE DID WITH WHAT WE KNEW (THOSE WHO EARNESTLY SEEK GOD WILL FIND HIM)

Ken Boa, one of my favorite authors and theologians, says, "There are two groups of people in the world: Those who are seeking to know God and those who are not; and in the end, both will be successful!"

C. S. Lewis said something similar in his book *The Great Divorce*.

"There are only two kinds of people in the end: those who say to God, 'Thy will be done,' and those to whom God says, in the end, 'Thy will be done.' All that are in Hell, choose it. Without that self-choice, there could be no Hell. No soul that seriously and constantly desires joy will ever miss it. Those who seek, find. To those who knock, it is opened."

What both quotes point out is one of the great megathemes of the Bible: God will judge us according to what we did with what we knew. That is, each will be judged based on his or her response to the revelation about God he or she was given.

Now I want to say this up front: I believe the Bible teaches very clearly that no one will be saved—live with God, angels, and righteous saints forever—unless he or she has bent the knee or expressed a repentant faith to the person of Jesus Christ. Here are some passages that are very clear on this:

> For God so loved the world that he gave his one and only Son, that whoever believes in him shall not perish but have eternal life. For God did not send his Son into the world to condemn the world, but to save the world through him. Whoever believes in him is not condemned, but whoever does not believe stands condemned already because he has not believed in the name of God's one and only Son. (John 3:16–18 NIV)

> Whoever believes in the Son has eternal life, but whoever rejects the Son will not see life, for God's wrath remains on him. (John 3:36 NIV)

> Jesus answered, "I am the way and the truth and the life. No one comes to the Father except through me." (John 14:6 NIV)

> Salvation is found in no one else, for there is no other name under heaven given to men by which we must be saved. (Acts 4:12 NIV)

> For there is one God and one mediator between God and men, the man Christ Jesus. (1 Tim. 2:5 NIV)

How and when this opportunity to bend the knee comes to a person has many possibilities, and scripture leaves them ambiguous. But what scripture clearly affirms is that it's of supreme importance what we do with the light we receive.

> Woe to you, Korazin! Woe to you, Bethsaida! If the miracles that were performed in you had been performed in Tyre and Sidon, they would have repented long ago in sackcloth and ashes. But I tell you, it will be more bearable for Tyre and Sidon on the Day of Judgment than for you. And you, Capernaum, will you be lifted up to the skies? No, you will go down to the depths. If the miracles that were performed in you had been performed in Sodom, it would have remained to this day. But I tell you that it will be more bearable for Sodom on the Day of Judgment than for you. (Matt. 11:21–24 NIV)

Jesus said here that the Tyrians and Sidonians will justly perish in their sin, though; if they had had more supernatural evidences, they would have repented (although we cannot be sure their repentance would have been permanent). But God isn't obligated to provide what we don't seek.

In his book *Against the Flow*, John Lennox says, "Christ solemnly comments on the fact that people have rejected him, in spite of having seen many of his mighty works. He indicates that the sentence will vary according to opportunity and privilege." [1]

Romans 2:5–8 (NIV) says, "God 'will give to each person

according to what he has done.' To those who by persistence in doing good seek glory, honor and immortality, he will give eternal life. But for those who are self-seeking and who reject the truth and follow evil, there will be wrath and anger."

Acting on the knowledge we have is of utmost importance, not only to those who don't yet believe but also for those who are followers of Jesus, because this can affect our rewards in heaven.

Matthew 25:20–23 (parable of the talents) teaches that we will be rewarded according to what we did with the resources God gave us.

Luke 19:12–27 (parable of the ten minas) teaches us that if we are true disciples of Jesus, we will bear fruit. If we don't bear fruit, "even what we have will be taken away" (v. 26); and if we do bear fruit, what we have will be multiplied. This is what I refer to as "kingdom economics"—return on investment beyond any reasonable expectations. But we must make the investment and put to use what we have been given by acting on the knowledge and resources we have been given.

What are these rewards? Only Jesus knows this for sure, but we are clearly able to "store up treasures in heaven" (Mat. 6:20 NIV), and the things that immediately come to mind when I think of what I might be able to send or store in heaven are relationships. Clearly, the more people we have invested in here, the more gratifying it is going to be to fellowship with them there. Ken Boa said, "Relationships are the currency of heaven!" Our wealth there will be the number of people we befriended here.

We will all have the reward of being with Jesus … *with Jesus*! This is the greatest reward anyone can receive, and this reward is by grace alone, received by a repentant faith alone. But there is also the possibility of some people having greater capacity and greater responsibilities for service (as taught by the parables of the talents and minas).

WHAT ABOUT THOSE WHO NEVER HEARD THE GOSPEL?

One question I am often asked (one of the top-ten apologetic questions), is: "What about those who never heard the gospel—never heard about Jesus?"

The question has a false assumption—that there may be some people who didn't receive enough information to be held accountable for their lack of pursuit of God.

A passage we used earlier, Acts 17:26–27, says we were born in a time and place that would give us the best opportunity to "seek for Him, even grope for Him, and find Him." So we can rule out when and where we were born, who our parents were or are, and what neighborhood we grew up in. These details were all ordained before the foundation of the world to provide us with the best opportunity to come to know God.

So, is there anyone who wasn't given enough information?

Scripture is clear; God gave us three revelations of Himself. I will call each of the revelations a "book." God has given us three books.

"Book one" is general revelation.

> The heavens declare the glory of God;
> the skies proclaim the work of his hands.
> Day after day they pour forth speech;
> night after night they display knowledge.
> There is no speech or language
> where their voice is not heard.
> Their voice goes out into all the earth,
> their words to the ends of the world.
> In the heavens he has pitched a tent for the sun.
> (Ps. 19:1–4 NIV)

> For since the creation of the world God's invisible qualities—his eternal power and divine nature—have been clearly seen, being understood from what has been made, so that men are without excuse. (Rom. 1:20 NIV)

This book is available to all people who have ever lived, no matter where or when they lived. All have looked into the heavens, and the thought has crossed their minds. How or who? What they did with this thought over time could have eternal significance to them. They were receiving knowledge, information, and to not respond to this leaves them "without excuse." God isn't obligated to reveal more information to us when we don't respond to what He has already given.

"Book two" is special revelation.

> All Scripture is God-breathed and is useful for teaching, rebuking, correcting, and training in righteousness, so that the man of God may be thoroughly equipped for every good work. (2 Tim. 3:16–17 NIV)

> Jesus replied, "Are you not in error because you do not know the Scriptures or the power of God?" (Mark 12:24 NIV)

God's word has been given to us as special revelation about Himself and His ways. When we have this available to us and don't pursue the knowledge within it, we are "without excuse."

"Book three" is personal revelation.

This is the book that is often forgotten. The book of personal revelation is Jesus Himself revealing Himself to someone who is seeking Him. Consider the disciples on the road to Emmaus. Luke 24:15 (NIV) says, "As they talked and discussed these things with each other, Jesus himself came up and walked along with them."

There was a Roman centurion who heard of Jesus and wanted to know more about Him. Acts 10:22 (NIV) says, "The men replied, 'We have come from Cornelius the centurion. He is a righteous and God-fearing man, who is respected by all the Jewish people. A holy angel told him to have you come to his house so that he could hear what you have to say.'"

God sent an angel to the centurion and Peter to bring them together so the centurion and his household could hear about Jesus.

There are many, many verified accounts today of people questioning their faith and asking God to reveal to them the truth of who He is. God honored their request through divine visitation, dreams, visions, or a follower of Jesus specifically sent to them.

Here is a submegatheme: God offers more revelation when we respond to the revelation He has already given us. Mark 4:25 (NIV) says, "To those who have ears to hear, more revelation of the kingdom will be given, but to those who do not have ears to hear, even what revelation they have been given will be taken away, or will prove ineffective."

Everyone has book one available to him or her. How we respond to book one determines God's response to us. Many who have responded to book one were then given access to books two and/or three.

In the end, people won't be in hell because they didn't have the Bible to read or someone to tell them about Jesus. They will be separated from God because they chose to ignore (show contempt for) the truth about God that was made available to them. All were given book one, all had book two, and all had book three available to them if they responded to book one. We aren't alone in finding God based on all this information; the Holy Spirit is at work, drawing us toward God and repentance. Ultimately, we aren't just making a bad decision with the information given, but we are rejecting the Holy Spirit, who is at work in our lives.

The scriptures are clear. "You will seek me and find me when you seek me with all your heart" (Jer. 29:13).

When we recognize something to be true, adjusting our attitudes and actions to conform to that truth is obedience; any other response— delaying, showing partial obedience, or seeking alternative truths—is disobedience (sin) and will affect either our eternal destiny or our rewards.

All scripture speaks of a God who says, "Knock and it will be opened to you; seek and you shall find" (Rev. 7:7). I believe as

Abraham did when he questioned God on His decision to destroy all in Sodom and Gomorrah. "Will not the Judge of all the earth do right?" (Gen. 18:25 NIV)

Scripture says that when we stand before God, we will have no excuses for the judgment He renders. The God of all the earth will do right, and He will judge us according to what we did with what we knew.

CHRISTLIKENESS IS OUR GOAL

What does living a life for Jesus look like? What can we expect to encounter as we desire to follow Jesus and His teachings? How do we become more like Jesus in our walk with Him? This chapter offers some megathemes to inform and encourage us toward our goal of Christlikeness.

MEGATHEME 11:

HOLINESS, NOT HAPPINESS, IS GOD'S PRIORITY FOR US

Many people who profess to be Christians—followers of Jesus—believe that if they become a Christian, life will go better for them; they will be happier because they are now "saved." I once taught a series on the top 10 lies of Satan! Satanic lie number one was, "It will go well with you once you become a Christian." What can we expect if we sincerely want to follow Jesus and be His disciple?

SCRIPTURES ON HOLINESS AND SANCTIFICATION

We are called to be holy. First Corinthians 1:2 (NIV) says, "To the church of God in Corinth, to those sanctified in Christ Jesus and called to be holy, together with all those everywhere who call on the name of our Lord Jesus Christ—their Lord and ours."

God chose us before the creation of the world to be holy and blameless. Do you feel blameless or holy? Does this seem like an impossible state of being?

> For he chose us in him before the creation of the world to be holy and blameless in his sight. (Eph. 1:4 NIV)

> But now he has reconciled you by Christ's physical body through death to present you holy in his sight, without blemish and free from accusation. (Col 1:22 NIV)

Yet this is an attainable state because Paul said he and those with him were "holy, righteous, and blameless" when they visited the Thessalonians. "You are witnesses, and so is God, of how holy, righteous and blameless we were among you who believed" (1 Thess. 2:10 NIV).

All of us can achieve this state because Jesus said that on the day of His return, He will be glorified "in His holy people … This includes you." "On the day he comes to be glorified in his holy people and to be marveled at among all those who have believed. This includes you, because you believed our testimony to you" (2 Thess. 1:10 NIV).

Yet even though we are called to a holy life, we are also invited to join Paul and our Lord in "suffering for the Gospel." "So do not be ashamed to testify about our Lord, or ashamed of me his prisoner. But join with me in suffering for the Gospel, by the power of God, who has saved us and called us to a holy life—not because of anything we have done but because of his own purpose and grace. This grace was given us in Christ Jesus before the beginning of time" (2 Tim. 1:8–9 NIV).

From these few passages alone (and there are many more), we see that becoming a follower of Jesus doesn't promise a care-free, happy life, but it results in our becoming holy as Jesus is holy. Part of that process of becoming holy is to endure suffering for the sake of Christ, just as He endured suffering for our sake.

We have fallen prey to a satanic lie when we think becoming a follower of Jesus will lead us to a happier, wealthy, and carefree life. Those who teach these things may gain a wide following because it's an easy message to deliver, but they are setting up their followers for disappointment and disillusionment when they encounter the first set of difficult circumstances because they are followers of Jesus.

Do you still want to be a disciple of Jesus? It doesn't come without cost (Luke 14:27–28).

WHAT IS HOLINESS?

First, we need to understand just what holiness is. Few of us have encountered the holiness of God. Here are some responses by those who have:

Jacob had a dream and saw angels ascending and descending on a ladder with "the Lord" standing at the top of the ladder. Read about his response. "When Jacob awoke from his sleep, he thought, 'Surely the Lord is in this place, and I was not aware of it.' He was afraid and said, 'How awesome is this place! This is none other than the house of God; this is the gate of heaven'" (Gen. 28:16–17 NIV).

Consider Isaiah, who was given a glimpse of the Most Holy surrounded by winged Seraphs. Look at his response. "'Woe to me!' I cried. 'I am ruined! For I am a man of unclean lips, and I live among a people of unclean lips, and my eyes have seen the King, the Lord Almighty'" (Isa. 6:5 NIV).

Ezekiel saw "visions of God" while in exile in Babylon. Here was his response. "Like the appearance of a rainbow in the clouds on a rainy day, so was the radiance around him. This was the appearance of the likeness of the glory of the Lord. When I saw it, I fell facedown, and I heard the voice of one speaking" (Ezek. 1:28 NIV).

Jesus just for a moment revealed His glory to those who came to arrest Him in the garden. Look at their response. "'Jesus of Nazareth,' they replied. 'I am he,' Jesus said. (And Judas the traitor was standing there with them.) When Jesus said, 'I am he,' they drew back and fell to the ground" (John 18:5–6 NIV).

John described a glimpse of the risen Christ in the opening of the book of Revelation. "When I saw him, I fell at his feet as though dead. Then he placed his right hand on me and said: 'Do not be afraid. I am the First and the Last. I am the Living One; I was dead, and behold I am alive for ever and ever! And I hold the keys of death and Hades'" (Rev. 1:17–18 NIV).

Clearly, when we encounter holiness, it is so totally "other than" what we are that we are fearful, retreating and desiring to prostrate ourselves before the One who is holy.

What is holiness?

The word or concept first appeared during creation when God set the seventh day apart from all the rest and declared it to be "holy" (Gen. 2:3). So there is an attribute of being set apart from all the rest.

Next, we see the word in Exodus when Moses encountered God on Mount Horeb. God said He was standing on "holy ground" and needed to remove his sandals to avoid defiling the ground on which he stood (Ex. 3:5–6). Moses then hid his face because he was afraid to look on God's holiness. We see in the introduction of holiness a purity, an absolute perfection, that is so "other than" its opposite (imperfection) that it's impossible for the imperfect to coexist with holiness. This may explain why the natural reaction of those who have encountered God's holiness is to draw back, retreat, cover their faces, and fall prostrate as though dead.

Here is one more description of holiness. When God informed Moses of His plans for the Israelites, He said, "Although the whole earth is mine, you will be for me a kingdom of priests and a holy nation" (Ex. 19:5–6).

God set Israel apart from the rest of the world. He wanted her to represent His otherness and perfection, and He didn't want her to coexist with her imperfect neighbors; thus, there was the eventual command to remove the Canaanites from the land Israel was to occupy.

If we were to now describe holiness as complete perfection, totally "other than" so that anything else is by any comparison imperfect, we can say holiness is the adjective that should be used in conjunction with all God's other attributes.

- God's love is a holy love; there is no other like it.
- God's mercy is a holy mercy, set apart from any other merciful act.
- God's anger is a holy anger, borne out of the desire and expectation of perfection and unwilling to compromise or coexist with something less.
- God's justice is a holy justice, perfect in its sentence and execution.

And can we try one more? God's jealousy is a holy jealousy. You have heard many times in scripture that our God is a "jealous God." At first, this doesn't sound complimentary. That is because our jealousy is most often unholy. We see a man or woman making advances toward someone we love, and we become jealous; that is, we feel threatened that someone is attempting to take from us what is ours.

A holy jealousy is quite different. This jealousy would love the beloved with a holy love, want only what is best for the beloved at all times, and would see the person making advances as a threat not to the observer's well-being but to the well-being of the beloved. Perhaps it may tempt him or her to actions that would bring painful consequences on the person and the ones he or she loves. And our response of anger wouldn't be in our self-interest but in the interest of the beloved.

God's jealousy is to protect not His reputation or property but the well-being of those He loves. This is why He was "jealous" when He saw the Israelites worshipping false gods or idols (Ex. 20:4).

This is the holiness God calls us to. It is a standard of perfection that is so "other than" its imperfect impostors that we are set apart and unable to coexist with any other standard. This now begs the question.

HOW DO WE BECOME HOLY?

This clearly is attainable since Jesus commanded us to be in this state. "Be perfect, therefore, as your heavenly Father is perfect" (Matt. 5:48 NIV).

Jesus didn't leave us with just the "what" we are to be; He also gave us the "how" in His conversation with the rich young ruler. "Jesus answered, 'If you want to be perfect, go, sell your possessions and give to the poor, and you will have treasure in heaven. Then come, follow me'" (Matt. 19:21 NIV).

To paraphrase: submit your life, possessions, and resources to Jesus and His kingdom's use of those things. We have already discussed how this cannot be done except by repentance.

Chuck Colson said, "At the cross there is a great exchange—an exchange of identities: 'Christ comes to the cross to die, giving His righteous life for us; we in turn come to the cross to die, surrendering our old sinful life for Him. Thereafter Christ lives in us'" (Gal. 2:20).[2]

Through a repentant faith, we come to the cross of Jesus and surrender our way of doing things, our resources, and our lives; Jesus meets us there and clothes us in His righteousness, making us holy at that moment and forever in the sight of the Father. But all of us who have made this trip to the cross know there is still a rebellious nature within us, one that wants the things of God, even God Himself, until He asks us to do something we don't naturally want to do. This nature must be taught to conform to Jesus's nature, so while we are perfect (holy), we are being perfected (made holy); and Jesus gives us His Spirit to accomplish this, even assuming the responsibility for making it so.

"Being confident of this, that he who began a good work in you will carry it on to completion until the day of Christ Jesus" (Phil. 1:6 NIV). Being holy begins with repentance and is made complete through obedience to what the Spirit asks us to do. This is one of those "both ands" of scripture we referred to earlier: two truths that must not be resolved but held in tension. We are both perfect and being made perfect at the same time.

Knowing God might ask us to do things that would cost us greatly or cause us to endure pain and suffering begs the question.

CAN I BE HAPPY AND A FOLLOWER OF JESUS AT THE SAME TIME?

Jesus wants to give us something much more valuable than happiness. Happiness is that pleasant feeling we experience when a need or desire is satisfied, like when we sit down to a good meal when we are hungry, are able to purchase a car when we need transportation, or get a letter saying we have been accepted into a program or school we applied for.

But this happiness is always fleeting; the positive, euphoric feelings begin to subside almost immediately after their onset. And soon we are looking for the next opportunity to experience happiness. We can become addicted to activities, things, or people who provide this "fix" for us. We wish we could experience happiness continuously, but it evades us. We want something more than happiness, but we don't know what we're seeking.

There is something more than happiness, and that's joy. Joy is the deep-seated conviction that all is well. Joy is the assurance that, despite our present circumstances, all will turn out for our long-term good. Joy is what we feel when our two emotional needs, significance and security, have been and are being met. (Look for more on this in a later chapter).

Jesus isn't about making us happy, which is momentary and transient. He is about giving us joy, which is permanent and resilient. Here is the example He set for us: "Let us fix our eyes on Jesus, the author and perfecter of our faith, who for the joy set before him endured the cross, scorning its shame, and sat down at the right hand of the throne of God" (Heb. 12:2 NIV).

Even when faced with His greatest trial—a painful, agonizing death—Jesus focused on the "joy set before him," a deep inner conviction that all was well. He believed His suffering would result in long-term good for millions or even billions of people and that His present circumstances were from His Father's hands and that His Father was pleased with Him. He couldn't have been more significant or securely loved than He was at that very time, the time of His trial, and He embraced His circumstances, rejecting the shame en route to taking His place beside His Father in the throne room of heaven.

Paul also learned from Jesus and gave this challenging but comforting passage: "I know what it is to be in need, and I know what it is to have plenty. I have learned the secret of being content in any and every situation, whether well fed or hungry, whether living in plenty or in want. I can do everything through him who gives me strength" (Phil. 4:12–13 NIV).

Paul didn't pursue happiness, but he pursued "being content in any and every situation." This is joy, the deep-seated conviction that all is well despite your circumstances.

CONCLUSION

Holiness is God's priority for us, and this isn't intended so we can't be happy but so we can experience joy, even when we face difficult and painful circumstances. God wants much more for us than happiness; He wants us to experience the joy of His presence in each and every moment in our lives forever and ever and ever. "To him who is able to keep you from falling and to present you before his glorious presence without fault and with great joy" (Jude 1:24 NIV).

MEGATHEME 12:

THE DESERT IS OFTEN GOD'S "FURNACE" TO PURIFY US, TO MAKE US HOLY

We just finished discussing that God wants us to become holy, transformed into the image of His Son. We said that after a repentant faith we are both declared holy and placed in the process of becoming holy (two truths to be held in tension). But now a more profound megatheme of scripture arises. The "desert" is often God's crucible to purify us, to make us holy.

In his *Thoughts for Life's Journey*, the late George Matheson of Scotland reechoed this discipline of despair. "My soul, reject not the place of thy prostration! It has ever been the robing room for royalty."[3] The desert is often God's robing room for glory.

What does this mean—the desert? We need to look at scripture to find some examples of people who found the desert to be their classroom for holiness, their "robing room for royalty."

EXAMPLES OF DESERT EXPERIENCES IN SCRIPTURE AND THEIR RESULTS

Moses in the Desert for Forty Years

Moses was approximately forty years old when he left Egypt (Acts 7:23), and he stayed in Midian approximately forty years (Acts 7:30). What did God accomplish in his life during this period?

We know Moses fled to Midian after killing an Egyptian who was beating an Israelite slave (Ex. 2:15). Moses had come to understand that the Israelites were his own people (Ex. 2:11) and thought this act would somehow endear him to them; perhaps he could help them in their plight (Acts 7:25). He was forty years old, a son of Egypt as well as a son of Israel. No doubt the finest tutors in Egypt had taught him as the adopted son of the Pharaoh's daughter. He probably saw power as the way to achieve success or change, and his instincts to kill the Egyptian would suggest this as well.

Yet when Moses emerged from the desert, the following was said of him: "(Now Moses was a very humble man, more humble than anyone else on the face of the earth)" (Num. 12:3 NIV).

What happened?

I'm sure that there were many nights, while Moses was tending to Jethro's sheep, that he looked up at the sky and asked God, "What is this all about? Why did You raise me among royalty, give me the ability to speak in front of kings, give me a heart for leadership and a passion to make a difference in the lives of people, and then send me to this desert to tend sheep? What is this all about? Lord, what is this all about?"

Have you ever felt this way? Have you ever wondered why you have been given talents and desires that aren't being used and are frustrated that you have been assigned to "this," your equivalent to tending sheep?

I believe as the years progressed and Moses was faithful to his duties as a shepherd, raising his family and learning to serve Jethro and his household, he began to see in this the contentment that comes from humble service. I believe there was one night, a night when there was a desert sky full of bright, beautiful, twinkling stars, when Moses looked up to the heavens and said, "Lord, thank You for all You have given me, and for this place You have brought me to serve You; and Lord, I still don't know what all that was about in Egypt, but if all You ever want me to do is to tend sheep in the desert, that is okay. I will tend Your sheep." That was the night Moses became qualified to be Israel's shepherd. Gratitude had replaced ambition, humility had replaced power, and serving now trumped leading. The desert was Moses's robing room for royalty—kingdom royalty.

The Children of Israel in the Desert for Forty Years

Israel had been miraculously rescued from Pharaoh's army. He witnessed God's holiness at Mount Sinai through the giving of the law and had been led by God through a cloud by day and a pillar of fire at night. They were brought to the edge of Canaan, and there they faltered after the report of the twelve spies that there were walled cities and giants in the land. Here was their response:

"That night all the people of the community raised their voices and wept aloud. All the Israelites grumbled against Moses and Aaron, and the whole assembly said to them, 'If only we had died in Egypt! Or in this desert! Why is the Lord bringing us to this land only to let us fall by the sword? Our wives and children will be taken as plunder. Wouldn't it be better for us to go back to Egypt?' And they said to each other, 'We should choose a leader and go back to Egypt'" (Num. 14:1–4 NIV).

And here was God's response: "For forty years—one year for each of the forty days you explored the land—you will suffer for your sins and know what it is like to have me against you" (Num. 14:34 NIV).

Sometimes the desert can be in response to disobedience. But it is still God's crucible to prepare us for greater service. During this next forty years, a generation perished that had known the hardships and comforts of Egypt. And in their place was raised a generation that knew how to survive in the desert, was at home in the desert, and depended on God even for their daily sustenance (manna). This generation was ready to go and conquer the land they had been given. When Joshua told them it was time to move out and cross the Jordan, look at the response: "Then they answered Joshua, 'Whatever you have commanded us we will do, and wherever you send us we will go'" (Josh. 1:16 NIV).

What did the desert do for Israel? Instead of a people who said, "Let's go back to Egypt!" they became a people who said, "Wherever you send us we will go!" This is the work of the desert; it is God's crucible for holiness.

David's Fleeing Saul for Eight Years

In 1 Samuel 21–31 and 2 Samuel 1, we learn that David was in the desert about eight years, fleeing Saul. He was about twenty-two to thirty years old during this period. Saul hunted David for four years (1018–1014 BC, and David was in Ziklag about four years (1014–1010 BC).

Like Moses, David must have wondered why he had to endure that experience. Samuel had appointed him to be king of Israel; he had killed the Philistine champion, Goliath, when all others had shrunk away from the challenge; and he had been a loyal servant to Saul—even marrying his daughter, Michal. Why must he now hide like a criminal in the desert, always being on guard against the armies of Saul, who were in constant pursuit of him?

Here are some of the experiences David had while in his desert (read 1 Samuel 21 and 2 Samuel 1; see some of David's growth experiences):

- David ate the consecrated bread, which Jesus later referenced (1 Sam. 21:1–6).
- He took possession of Goliath's sword, reminding him of God's anointing on him even while he was fleeing Saul (1 Sam. 21:9).
- The Lord brought a ragtag band of men, who would become known as "David's mighty men" (2 Sam. 23:8), to David at the cave of Adullam (1 Sam. 22:2).
- A priest of God, Abiathar, joined David's men, signifying God was with them (1 Sam. 22:20).
- David defeated the Philistines at Keilan—again confirming God's presence with him (1 Sam. 23:5).
- David demonstrated patience to wait for God's timing on his kingship by sparing Saul's life twice (1 Sam. 24; 26).
- David found a bride, Abigail (1 Sam. 25); the significance of this will be discussed later.
- David lived among the Philistines and learned their culture and tactics, which he would later use to defeat them (1 Sam. 27).
- David defeated the Amalekites, another confirmation that God was with him (1 Sam. 30).
- David killed the messenger who thought he was doing David a service by killing a wounded Saul and bringing David the crown from his head. This showed how much David respected the office of king, regardless of who held it and showing he was ready to be king (2 Sam. 1).

Consider the significance of David finding a bride, Abigail, in the desert. Jesus was rejected by his kinsmen (the Jews), went to a different people (the Gentiles), found a "bride" (the church), and will return one day to be the redeemer of His people, Israel. We have seen this pattern before in the Old Testament, when God used the lives of others to project the path the Messiah would walk.

Joseph was rejected by his kinsmen (his brothers), went to a different people (the Egyptians), found a bride (Asenath), and returned to Canaan as the savior of his brothers (taking them from a land of famine to a land of plenty).

Moses was rejected by his kinsmen (Israelites condemned him for killing the Egyptian), went to a different people (Jethro in Midian), found a bride (Zipporah), and returned to Egypt as the savior of his people (redeeming them from slavery).

David was rejected by his brothers (Saul, a Benjamite, and his own brothers from the tribe of Judah), went to a different people (Desert of Maon, where there was a Calebite, Nabal), found a bride (Abigail), and returned to his people (all the tribes of Israel) to become king over all Israel. Finding Abigail in the desert made David a type of Christ, something that may never have happened apart from the desert.

The desert shaped David, prepared him for the challenges that lay ahead for him as king, and assured him of God's anointing on his life. It was a place of prostration, and a robing room for royalty.

Jesus in the Desert for Forty Days

We know well the story of Jesus and the temptations He faced in the desert after His baptism by John. I don't want to do an exegesis of scripture here on the temptations of Christ, but I do want to point out something very significant about this experience for Jesus.

God chose Israel to be a people through whom God would reveal Himself to the world and bring salvation to it. Born in Canaan (Jacob was born in Canaan, in the land of the Hittites; Gen. 25:7–11), Israel fled to Egypt to avoid death (Jacob and sons moved to Egypt to avoid the famine and live with Joseph where there was plenty). They left Egypt, where they passed through the Red Sea (a type of baptism) under Moses and then entered the desert, where they were tested and made ready to enter Canaan. There they endured and became the "savior to the world" (through the birth of Jesus).

Let's summarize: Israel was born in Canaan under threat of death. He fled to Egypt, went through baptism in the Red Sea, and entered the desert for testing before entering Canaan to become savior to the world. Sound familiar?

Jesus was born in Canaan (Bethlehem) under threat of death. He fled to Egypt with his parents to escape Herod's edict to kill all baby boys under two years of age. He underwent baptism (in the Jordan by John the Baptist) before going into the desert for testing and then entering His kingdom as the Savior of the world.

Many have questioned why Jesus wanted to be baptized. He certainly didn't need to be baptized to cleanse Himself of sin. He said this needed to be done because "it is proper for us to do this to fulfill all righteousness" (Matt. 3:15). Perhaps one reason for this was to ensure He fit the template of Christ, which the life of the nation and people of Israel had established.

In the desert, Jesus was tempted three times, and each temptation strengthened Him and prepared Him for his ministry to come, just as Israel, Moses, and David before Him were strengthened. The desert was His "robing room for royalty."

What Are Some Deserts We Might Experience?

I don't know what kind of desert you might be facing as you read this. Perhaps these are a few:

- You have been working a job that meets your financial needs but leaves you unfulfilled in regard to your spiritual gifts or God-given passions.
- You are experiencing a long drought of success in your vocation.
- You have been rejected by someone you love, and the hurt continues without relief.

- You have been dealing with disappointment for a long time, and there is no end in sight.
- You feel cut off from God and don't have the assurance that He cares about you.

Take heart; you may be in a very special place. God may be preparing you for a work to come. He most definitely knows where you are and what you are experiencing, and He is orchestrating your circumstances for good (Rom. 8:28).

I once heard Ravi Zacharias say, "Never confuse pain and suffering for a lack of God's blessing, for through pain and suffering we come to know God better, and that is the greatest blessing of all."

Everyone in scripture who suffered a dark night of the soul—a desert—came to know God better and emerged from the experience stronger and better equipped for the service God had called him or her to. The desert is "God's robing room for glory!"

MEGATHEME 13:

THE ENEMY OF GOD'S BEST IS GOOD

"When the woman saw that the fruit of the tree was good for food and pleasing to the eye, and also desirable for gaining wisdom, she took some and ate it. She also gave some to her husband, who was with her, and he ate it" (Gen. 3:6 NIV).

Excursions into good things often derail our journey to holiness (God's best for us). And this is not by accident. It has been Satan's practice since the temptation of Eve in the garden to offer us good things to keep us from experiencing God's best.

Satan even tried this template on Jesus. "The tempter came to him and said, 'If you are the Son of God, tell these stones to become bread'" (Matt. 4:3 NIV).

Jesus was hungry. He was on a Father-ordained fast, one He could have ended at any time. Satan merely suggested that He could turn the stones into bread to satisfy His hunger. What could be the harm in this? How could this be a bad thing? On the surface, it seemed like a harmless, even compassionate, suggestion.

But Jesus saw through the offer of immediate self-gratification and recognized there was a purpose in maintaining His fast: being in communion with His Father to receive from His Father what the Father was willing to give Him to sustain Him for the duration of His earthly ministry. He refused Satan's offer, suggesting there was something better than physical bread, the life-giving word of God, which suggested He should continue His fast until the Father ordained it to be over. "Jesus answered, 'It is written: "Man does not live on bread alone, but on every word that comes from the mouth of God"'" (Matt. 4:4 NIV).

Jesus received something far better than "hot-n-now bread." The angels, God's best, attended to Him. "Then the devil left him, and angels came and attended him" (Matt. 4:11 NIV).

This pattern repeats itself in scripture. Men and women opt for a choice that appears to be good or even within God's plan for them, only to miss out on God's best because they didn't wait on God's timing for them to have what they desired and He desired for them.

Twice in my life, I can point to career choices that were made because a very good option had suddenly been presented to me. Being offered more responsibility, more income, better benefits, and so forth must be from God, right?

After a few months in both new positions, I found myself in difficult circumstances; my family life and prayer/study life were being suffocated by the demands of these new ventures. I went to the Lord in prayer and asked why He was allowing me to suffer these difficult conditions. His response was, "You never asked Me!"

I immediately asked God to open a door for me to return to the path He had chosen for me. In one case, He returned me to the exact point of my departure; in the other, He affirmed me in my position and encouraged me to press on and trust Him for the outcome.

I am sorry to say that I could make the same mistake twice, but this temptation to embrace good without asking God for His best is very subtle. We just assume all good things must be from God, but they may well be from the enemy to distract us from God's plan for our lives.

Here are several examples from scripture of people missing out on God's best by opting for what's good.

Abraham Takes Sarah's Counsel to Take Hagar

"Now Sarai, Abram's wife, had borne him no children. But she had an Egyptian maidservant named Hagar; so she said to Abram, 'The Lord has kept me from having children. Go, sleep with my maidservant; perhaps I can build a family through her'" (Gen. 16:1–2 NIV).

God had promised Abraham an heir—a son—but still none had been born to Sarah. On the surface, Sarah's counsel seemed good, even within God's plan; and Abraham accepted her counsel and slept with Hagar, who bore him a son, Ishmael.

The trouble that followed is the stuff novels and movies are made of. But just the scene where Abraham had to send Hagar and Ishmael, a woman and son whom he loved, into the desert, never to see them again, is heart wrenching. This never needed to happen, nor the events that have followed to this day from Abraham's bad decision. How different it might have been if Abraham had said to Sarah, "Thank you for your concern for me and our family, but I will consult with God on this before taking any further action."

Joshua's Defeat at Ai

Joshua and the Israelites had just experienced a great victory over Jericho, with God intervening miraculously on their behalf to bring down the great wall of the city. Before them was the small town of Ai. This was a small fly compared to the great beast of Jericho, which they handily defeated. So Joshua sent out a few spies to survey Ai and report back. "When they returned to Joshua, they said, 'Not all the people will have to go up against Ai. Send two or three thousand men to take it and do not weary all the people, for only a few men are there'" (Josh. 7:3 NIV).

"No problem!" they said. "Just send a small force and the city will be ours!" It sounded good to Joshua, and there was no record of him bringing the matter before God to get His instructions. The result was disastrous. "So about three thousand men went up; but they were routed by the men of Ai, who killed about thirty-six of them" (Josh. 7:4–5 NIV).

Now Joshua prostrated himself before God and discovered there was sin in the camp of Israel; someone has kept contraband from the destruction of Jericho. I believe it is reasonable to suggest that if Joshua had asked for God's thoughts on the destruction of Ai before taking the advice of his counselors, he would have discovered this issue without the loss of thirty-six lives. He missed God's best because he opted for good.

Jephthah's Vow

Here is a tragic story, a great example of scripture recording things as they happened, not necessarily as God wanted them to happen. It is a story of how two wrongs don't make a right

Jephthah has been selected to lead Israel on a campaign against its enemies; it was a campaign in which he would be successful. Before he headed into battle, he did something. "And Jephthah made a vow to the Lord: 'If you give the Ammonites into my hands, whatever comes out of the door of my house to meet me when I return in triumph from the Ammonites will be the Lord's, and I will sacrifice it as a burnt offering'" (Judg. 11:30–31 NIV).

Sounds great, doesn't it? How could God possibly disapprove of such thinking and commitment? Jephthah saw this as good—it must be pleasing to God—and set off without ever consulting God in this matter.

When he returned, he was mortified when what came out of his door to meet him was his daughter. "When he saw her, he tore his clothes and cried, 'Oh! My daughter! You have made me miserable and wretched, because I have made a vow to the Lord that I cannot break'" (Judg. 11:35 NIV).

Here is where, in my opinion, he made the second wrong. He assumed God wanted him to honor a vow God may not have been pleased with him making in the first place. Again, thinking that honoring the vow was good, he followed through on his commitment to sacrifice his daughter and suffered terrible grief and loss. What might have happened if he had repented of making such a rash vow and asked God's forgiveness and release from this vow? God detested the pagan practices of child sacrifice and most certainly would have stayed Jephthah's hand against his daughter, just as he'd stayed Abraham's hand against Isaac.

God's best was lost because of Jephthah's headlong, even rash, pursuit of good.

The Ark Taken into Battle and Lost

In the days of Samuel and Eli the priest, the Israelites suffered many consecutive defeats at the hands of the Philistines. Then the elders of Israel had an idea. "When the soldiers returned to camp, the elders of Israel asked, 'Why did the Lord bring defeat upon us today before the Philistines? Let us bring the ark of the Lord's covenant from Shiloh, so that it may go with us and save us from the hand of our enemies'" (1 Sam. 4:3 NIV).

Sounds great! And with no further discussion, the ark was brought to the battlefield with no opposition from Eli. No one stopped to say, "What does God think of the idea?" Why should they? The idea sounded too good, so it must be God's plan. The result was disastrous; the ark was captured, and Eli's two sons died in battle.

Saul's Counsel from Advisers When the Spirit of God Departed from Him

After Samuel informed Saul that God had rejected him as king, an evil spirit came over Saul and tormented him (1 Sam. 16:14). Saul's advisers had an idea. "Saul's attendants said to him, 'See, an evil spirit from God is tormenting you. Let our lord command his servants here to search for someone who can play the harp. He will play when the evil spirit from God comes upon you, and you will feel better'" (1 Sam. 16:15–16 NIV).

Saul, who knew the presence of the Spirit of God, now felt the absence of that Spirit and the presence of an evil spirit. The advice he received? "Get someone to play a harp for you!" It sounds good, doesn't it? Surely there could be no harm in that. And David, the future king of Israel, was summoned to the king's court.

How much better if Saul, like David after he sinned, had fallen on his face before God and said,

> Create in me a pure heart, O God,
> and renew a steadfast spirit within me.
> Do not cast me from your presence
> or take your Holy Spirit from me.
> Restore to me the joy of your salvation
> and grant me a willing spirit, to sustain me.
> (Ps. 51:10–12 NIV)

What if Saul had repented and asked God to "restore to me the joy of your salvation"? That is, he asked God to come and commune with him again. Might Saul's story have been different if he had opted for God's best (God Himself) instead of good (temporary relief from an evil spirit)?

Samuel's Desire to Select Eliab over David as King

During this same time frame after God had rejected Saul as king, Saul sent Samuel to the house of Jesse to "anoint one of his sons as the future king of Israel" (1 Sam. 16:1). "When they arrived, Samuel saw Eliab and thought, 'Surely the Lord's anointed stands here before the Lord'" (1 Sam. 16:6 NIV).

Samuel was ready to pour the oil right then and there. Eliab must have been impressive; the oldest son was a fitting specimen to be king. Samuel was tempted to act on what was good, but God intervened. "But the Lord said to Samuel, 'Do not consider his appearance or his height, for I have rejected him. The Lord does not look at the things man looks at. Man looks at the outward appearance, but the Lord looks at the heart'" (1 Sam. 16:7 NIV).

Samuel didn't fall for good and miss out on God's best, but the temptation was present.

Rehoboam's Flawed Advisers

Solomon had been a hard taskmaster during his massive building projects while king. After his death, the people came to his son Rehoboam and said, "Your father put a heavy yoke on us, but now lighten the harsh labor and the heavy yoke he put on us, and we will serve you" (1 Kings 12:4 NIV).

Rehoboam sent them away and turned to his advisors, both the elders of Israel and a younger group more familiar to him. The elders "replied, 'If today you will be a servant to these people and serve them and give them a favorable answer, they will always be your servants'" (1 Kings 12:7 NIV).

But Rehoboam rejected their advice and turned to the younger advisors, who said to him, "Tell these people who have said to you, 'Your father put a heavy yoke on us, but make our yoke lighter'—tell them, 'My little finger is thicker than my father's waist. My father laid on you a heavy yoke; I will make it even heavier. My father scourged you with whips; I will scourge you with scorpions'" (1 Kings 12:10–11 NIV).

This sounded good to Rehoboam. After all, a king should be firm and authoritative, right? So he took this good advice and never asked God to help him decide between the two choices. His kingdom was ripped into two parts, and ten of the twelve tribes walked away from his kingship because of this decision. Rehoboam missed God's best by opting for what sounded to him like something good.

Hezekiah's "Temple Tour"

If you have a great temple, with many treasures, why not give a tour to traveling dignitaries? At least this is what Hezekiah thought.

Hezekiah had been a good king. God had recently honored his request to extend his life and had been given fifteen more years to reign. Having heard of his miraculous recovery, the king of Babylon sent gifts and envoys to Jerusalem to meet with Hezekiah. What better thing should one do to be a good host than to show off one of your most prized possessions and all within it?

"Hezekiah received the messengers and showed them all that was in his storehouses—the silver, the gold, the spices and the fine oil—his armory and everything found among his treasures. There was nothing in his palace or in all his kingdom that Hezekiah did not show them" (2 Kings 20:13 NIV).

Hezekiah, who had just had a magnificent moment with Isaiah and God on the matter of his health, never stopped to question this good thought he acted on. Isaiah received news of this and went to see him.

"Then Isaiah said to Hezekiah, 'Hear the word of the Lord: The time will surely come when everything in your palace, and all that your fathers have stored up until this day, will be carried off to Babylon. Nothing will be left, says the Lord. And some of your descendants, your own flesh and blood, that will be born to you, will be taken away, and they will become eunuchs in the palace of the king of Babylon'" (2 Kings 20:16–18 NIV).

How different the outcome might have been had Hezekiah sought God's best instead of good.

Peter's Concern for Jesus to Go to Jerusalem

We cannot leave this section without looking again at how Jesus handled the temptation to opt for good instead of what was best. We have already seen that Satan confronted Him with this in the desert.

Now Satan revisited Him again with the same strategy (and why not—it worked so well).

Jesus had begun to tell His disciples that He was to be killed and that they needed to go to Jerusalem. "Peter took him aside and began to rebuke him. 'Never, Lord!' he said. 'This shall never happen to you!'" (Matt. 16:22 NIV).

I don't know about you, but it would have sounded good to me to have someone I was very close to suggest that I didn't have to endure suffering that appeared inevitable. We can only be eternally grateful that our Lord saw the source of the offer, the opportunity to embrace good and miss the best.

"Jesus turned and said to Peter, 'Get behind me, Satan! You are a stumbling block to me; you do not have in mind the things of God, but the things of men'" (Matt. 16:23 NIV).

Jesus was focused on pursuing His Father's best for Himself and for us. What was Good was never an option for Him. How often we suffer consequences God never intended us to bear because we didn't take the time to question a good invitation to see whether it was really God's best for us.

MEGATHEME 14:

LIKE JESUS WE MUST PUT OUR DESIRES AND EXPECTATIONS ASIDE TO SHOULDER THE CIRCUMSTANCES OF OTHERS

"Let us fix our eyes on Jesus, the author and perfecter of our faith, who for the joy set before him endured the cross, scorning its shame, and sat down at the right hand of the throne of God" (Heb. 12:2 NIV).

Contrary to pursuing happiness, followers of Jesus must be willing to bear crosses and put their desires and expectations aside to shoulder the circumstances of another. This won't result in happy feelings, but it will bring joy and develop Christ like character.

Our Lord put aside any desires or expectations He might have had as a fully human man so He might shoulder the circumstances (a death sentence for sins) of His bride (the church). And He did this for the joy, the opportunity, and the privilege of being our Savior, our Redeemer.

If the Father expected this of His Son, why wouldn't He expect the same from His adopted sons and daughters? We have several examples in scripture of people who were asked to do this; they were types of Christ in that they put their desires and expectations aside to shoulder the circumstances of others.

Salmon and Rahab

We first encounter Rahab at Jericho. "Then Joshua son of Nun secretly sent two spies from Shittim. 'Go, look over the land,' he said, 'especially Jericho.' So they went and entered the house of a prostitute named Rahab and stayed there" (Josh. 2:1 NIV).

She was a prostitute, yet she had heard of the Israelites and that God had put His favor on them; she knew her city was doomed. She asked the Israelites to spare her and her family. "Now then, please swear to me by the Lord that you will show kindness to my family, because I have shown kindness to you. Give me a sure sign that you will spare the lives of my father and mother, my brothers and sisters, and all who belong to them, and that you will save us from death" (Josh. 2:12–13 NIV).

The spies agreed, and Rahab's house became salvation for all who would enter from the destruction of Jericho. But now what? What happened to a woman who had a past like Rahab in a nation that valued purity and holiness? What future could she possibly have had?

We must wait until the Gospel of Matthew to find out:

> Salmon the father of Boaz, whose mother was Rahab,
> Boaz the father of Obed, whose mother was Ruth,
> Obed the father of Jesse. (Matt. 1:5 NIV)

In the lineage of Christ, Rahab's name appears as the wife of a man named Salmon. When Rahab came into the camp of Israel, an object of scorn and shame, a man (Salmon) decided to put aside any desires he might have had for a more virtuous wife. He endured any shame he might have received from marrying a former prostitute, and he shouldered Rahab's circumstances so she might become the woman God had given her the potential to be.

Salmon was a type of Christ in that he voluntarily took on difficult circumstances for the benefit of another. And his actions had downstream benefits.

Boaz and Ruth

In the same passage above, we see that Salmon and Rahab are in the lineage of one named Boaz. This is the man who married Ruth the Moabitess.

We know Ruth's story. She is a Moabite woman who met one of the sons of Naomi when her husband and two sons went to Moab to escape harsh times in Israel.

Moab wasn't a friend to Israel. A nation that had its genesis from an incestuous relationship between Lot and one of his daughters (Gen. 19:37), Moab was a thorn in Israel's side from its beginnings. Through the council of Balak, the Moabite women seduced the men of Israel into sexual immorality and dietary sins (eating food sacrificed to idols) so they might lose favor with their God (Rev. 2:14).

The Moabites were a pagan people with pagan sexual practices, and Ruth was a product of this culture. To what degree Ruth embraced the practices of this culture, we don't know, but that she was a "Moabitess" put a mark on her purity.

Like Rahab, however, Ruth accepted God's provision for her redemption (escape with Naomi to Israel), and she too found herself in the midst of the Israelite culture as a widowed Moabitess.

The story of Ruth and Boaz is in the book of Ruth, and the story ends with Boaz becoming her "kinsman-redeemer" (Ruth 3:9). To do this, Boaz had to put aside any expectations he might have had for a more virtuous Israelite bride. He endured the shame any might try to put on him for marrying Ruth, and he shouldered her circumstances that she might become the woman God had given her the potential to be.

Both Rahab and Ruth are honored for their decisions to follow God's offer of provision for them, and they are listed in the lineage of Jesus, the Savior of the world. Both Salmon and Boaz give us a picture of our "kinsman-redeemer" to come. This is One who would put aside His desires and expectations to shoulder our circumstances.

Hosea and Gomer

This is perhaps one of my favorite biblical stories. It is a word picture of the redemptive work Christ would do for His bride, the church. I won't develop the entire story here, but for the purpose of supporting this megatheme, we need to know Hosea was a promising young prophet in Israel when he was asked to do something very painful. "When the Lord began to speak through Hosea, the Lord said to him, 'Go, take to yourself an adulterous wife and children of unfaithfulness, because the land is guilty of the vilest adultery in departing from the Lord'" (Hos. 1:2 NIV).

I won't debate here whether Gomer was adulterous before and/ or after their marriage, but what is clear is that God asked Hosea to marry a woman he knew would be unfaithful to him or one who had been promiscuous even before their marriage.

To marry Gomer, probably something he wanted to do out of love for her, Hosea had to put aside any desires for, or expectations of, a virtuous bride. He had to shoulder the shame and ridicule the culture would heap on him for her unfaithfulness. And God asked him to remain faithful to Gomer, even when she proved unfaithful to him.

"The Lord said to me, 'Go, show your love to your wife again, though she is loved by another and is an adulteress. Love her as the Lord loves the Israelites, though they turn to other gods and love the sacred raisin cakes'" (Hos. 3:1 NIV).

Hosea loved Gomer, and the end of this story is a beautiful word picture of reconciliation and a restored marriage. "Then I told her,

'You are to live with me many days; you must not be a prostitute or be intimate with any man, and I will live with you'" (Hos. 3:3 NIV).

Hosea put his desires and expectations aside to shoulder the circumstances (sins) of Gomer so she might become the woman God had intended her to be. In so doing, Hosea gave us a portrait of Christ to come, who will likewise shoulder His bride's (the church's) sins so she might become the bride she was intended to be.

Esther

Men are not the only ones asked to be like Christ. Esther was also asked to shoulder difficult circumstances so her people, the Jews, would be spared extinction and the Savior of the world would come from the remnant she saved.

Esther was just a young girl when she was taken into King Xerxes's harem to be evaluated as a candidate for queen to replace Queen Vashti, who refused to be paraded by the king in front of his male cohorts to show off her beauty. Esther won the beauty contest and became queen of Babylon.

I'm sure Esther had dreams of marrying a Jewish man and having children, who would fall under the Abrahamic covenant (Gen. 12:2–3). Instead, she was forcibly taken into the king's harem. Her desires and expectations were radically adjusted.

Later, Esther was made aware of a plot by a wicked man—Haman—to kill all the Jews in the kingdom. She had another tough decision to make. Approaching the king without invitation was risky; he could accept her or deny her, which would result in her death.

Esther decided to set her own desires and security aside to shoulder the circumstances (certain death) of her people. She approached the king at great risk to her person and interceded for her people, winning their ability to defend themselves and avoid their demise. In doing so, Esther became a type of Christ by putting her life at risk to approach the king, intercede for her people, and avoid their certain death. She gave us a beautiful picture of Christ to come.

Joseph and Mary

Lastly, there is Joseph, the human father of Jesus. He must have been an exemplary man for God to choose him to be the earthly father of the Son of God. He had met the woman he wanted to marry, and she was everything he had desired in a wife. And then she turned up pregnant.

Now, I know eventually Gabriel came and assured Joseph that Mary hadn't been unfaithful to him, but this still left the rest of the community. What did they think? And what they thought affected Joseph a great deal, because he would have to live in that community, a community that would think he'd violated his engagement by having sexual relations with Mary before they were married.

Joseph decided to put his desires (of a blemish-free reputation) aside and shoulder Mary's circumstances (pregnancy by the Holy Spirit) so she might be the woman God had intended her to be: the mother of the Son of God. Joseph became like Christ in his actions, foreshadowing the work of Christ to come.

Here's just a footnote on all the above. Not only do the people whose circumstances are shouldered become the people they were given the potential to be, but also the one who shouldered the circumstances fulfills his or her greatest potential. But isn't that just like a God who, when He acts, does the most good for the greatest number and for the longest period?

Crosses versus Thorns

There's another distinction here. We have been discussing crosses in this section, difficult circumstances that are voluntarily taken on for the benefit of another (and also ourselves). Many people confuse crosses with thorns.

Paul gave us the idea of a thorn when he prayed that his thorn might be removed. "To keep me from becoming conceited because of these surpassingly great revelations, there was given me a thorn in my flesh, a messenger of Satan, to torment me" (2 Cor. 12:7 NIV).

A thorn isn't something we choose to accept; it is given to us, even against our will. Paul prayed three times that his thorn would be removed, yet it wasn't. So, for the sake of distinction, a thorn is something unpleasant and undesirable God gave to us, but it is intended to produce a good outcome if we will bear it patiently and gladly. We will learn more about this when we discuss poisoned apples in a later chapter.

In contrast, a cross is something unpleasant we voluntarily take on our shoulders so someone else might benefit from our suffering. And we are to bear this gladly as well. "Then he said to them all: 'If anyone would come after me, he must deny himself and take up his cross daily and follow me'" (Luke 9:23 NIV).

If you want to be a true disciple of Jesus, you must be willing to set your desires and expectations aside to shoulder the circumstances of another—and to do so with joy, realizing two nail-scarred hands are clapping with every step you take.

What cross has Jesus asked you to shoulder? Does shouldering that cross bring shame on you in the eyes of others? If so, scorn the shame; that is, reject, despise, and refuse it, because this is to your glory, not your shame, to be like Jesus. And one day you will sit with Him and hear, "Well done, good and faithful servant!"

GOD HAS PROVIDED ALL WE NEED

> God can do this because He has no needs.
> I have no need of a bull from your stall
> or of goats from your pens,
> for every animal of the forest is mine,
> and the cattle on a thousand hills.
> (Ps. 50:9–10 NIV)

Our God owns "the cattle on a thousand hills." He needs nothing from us; He is not a God who needs His creation to self-actualize. He has no need of us whatsoever, but He invites us to enjoy His creation and participate in His redemptive work to reconcile all creation unto Himself.

It's important that we keep this in mind at all times. It may at first make us feel unimportant, but we are in fact very important to God; God just doesn't *need* us, and that is good news. Since He doesn't need us, He can love us unconditionally, with no expectations from us, only the desire that we would come to know Him and love Him freely. But this is God desire, not a need. We'll discuss this idea more fully later.

The fact that God doesn't need anything makes Him self-sufficient.

> Listen to me, O Jacob,
> Israel, whom I have called:

I am he;
I am the first and I am the last.
My own hand laid the foundations of the earth,
and my right hand spread out the heavens;
when I summon them,
they all stand up together.
(Isa. 48:12–13 NIV)

He is the image of the invisible God, the firstborn
over all creation. For by him all things were created:
things in heaven and on earth, visible and invisible,
whether thrones or powers or rulers or authorities; all
things were created by him and for him. He is before
all things, and in him all things hold together.
(Col. 1:15–17 NIV)

Self-sufficiency implies that God already has (or can create) anything He desires for His purposes. This is great news for you and me. This means for anything God asks us to do, He can provide for our needs to do it. And one of the great megathemes of scripture is that God has already provided all we need.

The Lord will guide you always;
he will satisfy your needs in a sun-scorched land
and will strengthen your frame.
You will be like a well-watered garden,
like a spring whose waters never fail.
(Isa. 58:11 NIV)

And my God will meet all your needs according to his
glorious riches in Christ Jesus. (Phil. 4:19 NIV)

The three megathemes that follow further develop this truth.

MEGATHEME 15:

GOD TRANSFORMS THE ORDINARY INTO THE EXTRAORDINARY

Henry Blackaby, in his book *Experiencing God*, says that after we receive a revelation from God, a calling to go or do a particular thing, we experience a "crisis of belief." "When God asks you to do something you cannot do, you will face a crisis of belief. You'll have to decide what you really believe about God. Can He and will He do what He has said He wants to do through you? Can God do the seemingly impossible through your ordinary life? How you respond to His invitation reveals what you truly believe about God, regardless of what you say." [4]

Most of us immediately feel inadequate, unqualified to attempt the task set before us. Consider Moses's response to returning to Egypt to bring the Israelites out of slavery and back to Canaan. "But Moses said to God, 'Who am I, that I should go to Pharaoh and bring the Israelites out of Egypt?'" (Ex. 3:11 NIV).

And even after God gave Moses specific instructions on what to do and affirmation that He, God, would go with him, Moses responded this way. "But Moses said, 'O Lord, please send someone else to do it'" (Ex. 4:13 NIV). And we are not much different. When God gives us a God-sized assignment, we most certainly feel inadequate for the task and experience a "crisis of belief."

But there is good news, God transforms the ordinary into the extraordinary, and that includes you.

Here are some well-known examples from scripture:

- Abraham (God chose a fearful man to become a pillar of faith)
- Joseph (the eleventh son of a sojourner became Egypt's prime minister)
- Moses (the infant son of a slave woman became prince of Egypt)

- Gideon (from the least of families in Manasseh came a deliverer)
- Ruth (a Moabite's widow became a mother of David and Christ)
- Samuel (born to a barren Levite woman, he became a judge of Israel)
- David (a shepherd became a mighty warrior and king of Israel)
- Daniel (an exile in Babylon rose to be prime minister of the land)
- Esther (an exile in Babylon became queen and savior of her people)
- John the Baptist (from a barren womb, he became "the Elijah who was to come" (Mat. 11:14 NIV))
- Mary (an obscure woman became the mother of God)
- The apostles (from common vocations to disciples, apostles of Jesus)

But since these stories are so well known, I thought I would pick a few lesser-known examples of God calling the ordinary and making them extraordinary.

BENAIAH, SON OF JEHOIADA

Benaiah was the son of Jehoiada, a priest. God gifted him to become a mighty warrior for David. In fact, he became one of David's "mighty men." Here is a brief description of his unique abilities: "Benaiah son of Jehoiada was a valiant fighter from Kabzeel, who performed great exploits. He struck down two of Moab's best men. He also went down into a pit on a snowy day and killed a lion. And he struck down a huge Egyptian. Although the Egyptian had a spear in his hand, Benaiah went against him with a club. He snatched the spear from the Egyptian's hand and killed him with his own spear.

Such were the exploits of Benaiah son of Jehoiada; he too was as famous as the three mighty men" (2 Sam. 23:20–22 NIV).

He also helped Solomon become king, killed Solomon's enemies, and served as the chief of Solomon's army. There is no other reason to expect Benaiah's success other than God called him from an ordinary background (son of a priest) and gifted him extraordinarily to do a special task.

THE WIDOW IN ZAREPHATH

Here was truly a common person of no special means or abilities. She was also a widow. Now Elijah fled from Jezebel, and the Lord sent him to the town of Zarephath. "Go at once to Zarephath of Sidon and stay there. I have commanded a widow in that place to supply you with food" (1 Kings 17:9 NIV).

This widow had God's attention, and God chose her to minister to the great prophet Elijah. Elijah went as directed and met the widow. He asked her for food. "'As surely as the Lord your God lives,' she replied, 'I don't have any bread—only a handful of flour in a jar and a little oil in a jug. I am gathering a few sticks to take home and make a meal for myself and my son, that we may eat it—and die'" (1 Kings 17:12 NIV).

Talk about being ordinary! This widow saw herself as subordinary because she was preparing a last meal for herself and her son. Elijah encouraged her to prepare a meal for him and trust that God would provide for her and for her son. She stepped out in faith and is witness to a miracle of creating food from scraps—her flour and oil didn't run dry all the while Elijah stayed with her and her son.

But there is more. She was witness to another great miracle: her son died, but Elijah restored him to life. How would you like to have had a front-row seat to Elijah and his relationship with God?

Centuries later, she isn't forgotten. Jesus remembered her as a representative of those to whom salvation would be offered after the Jews had rejected it. Elijah was a type of Christ to her; he brought life (salvation) to her when she was about to die and to her son when he died. Rejected by his own people (remember he was running from Jezebel), Elijah was then sent to a Gentile woman, where the glory of God was revealed to her. And Jesus remembered her. "Yet Elijah was not sent to any of them, but to a widow in Zarephath in the region of Sidon" (Luke 4:26 NIV).

An ordinary woman was given an extraordinary role in God's plan to bring salvation to the Gentiles.

THE HEBREW SLAVE GIRL IN NAAMAN'S HOUSEHOLD

This is my favorite example of an ordinary person being called to an extraordinary role. We are never given the name of this young slave girl; we are told only that she was in the house of Naaman. "Now Naaman was commander of the army of the king of Aram. He was a great man in the sight of his master and highly regarded, because through him the Lord had given victory to Aram. He was a valiant soldier, but he had leprosy. Now bands from Aram had gone out and had taken captive a young girl from Israel, and she served Naaman's wife. She said to her mistress, 'If only my master would see the prophet who is in Samaria! He would cure him of his leprosy'" (2 Kings 5:1–3 NIV).

This young girl was sovereignly placed in the household of the commander of the army of Aram. She knew about Elisha, and she had the courage, the faith, to believe Naaman would be healed if he met Elisha. This was a God-given faith and extraordinary gifting to an ordinary person. This young girl took on great risk that if Naaman acted on her words, went to Elisha, and wasn't healed, he might return and punish her and her family for her impudence.

Naaman acted on her suggestion, found Elisha, and was healed. "Then Naaman and all his attendants went back to the man of God. He stood before him and said, 'Now I know that there is no God in all the world except in Israel. Please accept now a gift from your servant'" (2 Kings 5:15 NIV).

We don't know the full impact of this powerful man, now a worshipper of Yahweh, returning home. An ordinary slave girl, whose name we don't know, but one day will, was gifted with the extraordinary, and this man and perhaps his household and beyond were blessed. God's ability to use ordinary people is extraordinary.

AMOS THE PROPHET

The book of Amos opens with these words: "The words of Amos, one of the shepherds of Tekoa" (Amos 1:1 NIV). Amos was a common shepherd; then God came to him. "But the Lord took me from tending the flock and said to me, 'Go, prophesy to my people Israel'" (Amos 7:15 NIV).

Amos was sent to the northern kingdom of Israel and there was told to point out to the people their sins and their need for repentance. His was a hard message, and he delivered it against tough opposition. "Then Amaziah the priest of Bethel sent a message to Jeroboam king of Israel: 'Amos is raising a conspiracy against you in the very heart of Israel. The land cannot bear all his words'" (Amos 7:10 NIV).

But Amos persisted in delivering his message that if the people didn't repent, God would send judgment on them as a nation. And the end of his book is a wonderful picture of the messianic kingdom, which Amos promised a remnant of Israel would survive to see. God wouldn't forget His covenant with Israel, but they could have avoided much pain and suffering if they had remained faithful to God.

I list Amos among the "ordinary made extraordinary" because I find it encouraging that God can and does take ordinary people and use them for extraordinary purposes.

THE SAMARITAN WOMAN AT THE WELL

A Samaritan woman, whose name we are never told, had an encounter with Jesus, and her less-than-ordinary life was transformed to an extraordinary one.

This woman had five husbands and was now living with a man who wasn't her husband. This is probably the reason she was at the well at midday instead of the cool of the day when most of the other women came to draw water. They no doubt chided her or shunned her for her heritage (Samaritan) and moral behavior. Then Jesus arrived.

There was a conversation between the woman and Jesus, which ended with Jesus revealing Himself to her to be the long-awaited Messiah. And she responded. "Then, leaving her water jar, the woman went back to the town and said to the people, 'Come, see a man who told me everything I ever did. Could this be the Christ?' They came out of the town and made their way toward him" (John 4:28–30 NIV).

She became the first female missionary for Jesus. She met Jesus, then went around her hometown and told them about His divinity. And they responded. "Many of the Samaritans from that town believed in him because of the woman's testimony, 'He told me everything I ever did.' So when the Samaritans came to him, they urged him to stay with them, and he stayed two days. And because of his words many more became believers. They said to the woman, 'We no longer believe just because of what you said; now we have heard for ourselves, and we know that this man really is the Savior of the world'" (John 4:39–42 NIV).

God took the ordinary and made her extraordinary.

THE MAN WHO HAD A LEGION OF DEMONS

A man, whose name we are never told, had a "legion" of demons within him, making him despicable to the local community. Jesus transformed him from subordinary to extraordinary.

Jesus exorcised the demons, and the man was left transformed into a new creature. "When they came to Jesus, they saw the man who had been possessed by the legion of demons, sitting there, dressed and in his right mind; and they were afraid" (Mark 5:15 NIV).

And he desired to follow Jesus, but he received a different ministry. "As Jesus was getting into the boat, the man who had been demon-possessed begged to go with him. Jesus did not let him, but said, 'Go home to your family and tell them how much the Lord has done for you, and how he has had mercy on you.' So the man went away and began to tell in the Decapolis how much Jesus had done for him. And all the people were amazed" (Mark 5:18–20 NIV).

Jesus equipped this man with an amazing testimony that made him an extraordinary evangelist for the good news.

MARY MAGDALENE

Here is another woman who was subordinary when we first meet her. "After this, Jesus traveled about from one town and village to another, proclaiming the good news of the kingdom of God. The Twelve were with him, and also some women who had been cured of evil spirits and diseases: Mary (called Magdalene) from whom seven demons had come out" (Luke 8:1–2 NIV).

Seven demons had possessed her; then she met Jesus, and her life was transformed. We find her

- at the cross (Mark 15:40);
- at the tomb when Jesus was buried (Matt. 27:61);
- at the tomb on Sunday, one of the first to see the stone rolled away (Matt 16:1);
- at the tomb on Sunday, the first to see the resurrected Jesus (Mark 16:9);
- as one of the first to tell the apostles about Jesus's resurrection (Luke 24:10; John 20;18).

Mary's was a subordinary life made extraordinary.

ONESIMUS THE SLAVE

Lastly, there is the slave of Philemon named Onesimus. We learn about him in a letter from Paul to Philemon, in which Paul described his former life like this: "Formerly he was useless to you" (Philem. 1:11 NIV).

It's hard to be more ordinary than that. He apparently ran away from Philemon, to whom he probably owed a debt. This may be the reason he entered service as a slave (this was a common practice in the Roman world).

But his flight led him to Paul and to an encounter with the gospel through Jesus. And his life was transformed. We see him mentioned in Colossians when Paul said he was sending someone with Tychicus to the Colossians to encourage them. He said, "He is coming with Onesimus, our faithful and dear brother, who is one of you. They will tell you everything that is happening here" (Col. 4:9 NIV).

Now Onesimus was a "faithful and dear brother," and Paul wrote Philemon to ask him to restore Onesimus—not just to repay his debt to him but also to consider that he may be more valuable now to him than ever. "Perhaps the reason he was separated from you for a little while was that you might have him back for good—no longer as a slave, but better than a slave, as a dear brother. He is very dear to me but even dearer to you, both as a man and as a brother in the Lord" (Philem. 1:15–16 NIV).

Thus, we see another transformed life.

Summary:

Benaiah, Son of Jehoiada

A priest's son became a mighty warrior and general of Solomon's army.

The Widow in Zarephath

A widow became witness to Elijah's ministry and was named by Jesus.

The Hebrew Slave Girl in Naaman's Household

A slave girl became the instrument of salvation to a Gentile nation.

Amos the Prophet

A lowly shepherd became a mighty prophet of God.

The Samaritan Woman at the Well

A shunned adulteress became the first woman missionary.

The Man Who Had a Legion of Demons

A despicable man was transformed into an ambassador for Jesus.

Mary Magdalene

A demon-possessed woman was the first to see the resurrected Christ.

Onesimus the Slave

A runaway slave was returned to his master as a brother in Christ. Yes, God transforms the ordinary into the extraordinary.

MEGATHEME 16:

OUR SIGNIFICANCE AND SECURITY ARE IN GOD ALONE

It has long been recognized that human beings have two emotional needs. First is the need for significance—to believe one's life has meaning or purpose. Second is the need for security—to believe one is loved and provided for without condition.

David recognized this when he wrote,

> My salvation and my honor depend on God;
> he is my mighty rock, my refuge.
> (Ps. 62:7 NIV)

My salvation (unconditional love and provision) and my honor (my significance) depend on God, according to David.

Scripture says God is the only One who can provide for these needs. First, the only One who can give us true security—who can love us unconditionally—is God.

> Praise the Lord, O my soul;
> all my inmost being, praise his holy name.
> Praise the Lord, O my soul,
> and forget not all his benefits—
> who forgives all your sins
> and heals all your diseases,
> who redeems your life from the pit
> and crowns you with love and compassion,
> who satisfies your desires with good things
> so that your youth is renewed like the eagle's.
> (Ps. 103:1–5 NIV)

This is a word picture of everlasting love or true security. And David succinctly declared his trust in God's security succinctly here.

> But I trust in you, O Lord;
> I say, "You are my God."
> My times are in your hands.
> (Ps. 31:14–15 NIV)

David placed his security completely in God's hands, because God had proved to David that He could be trusted. And God is also the One who gives us our significance. Scripture says we were made for a purpose, a unique purpose, assigned to us before the foundation of the world. "For we are God's workmanship, created in Christ Jesus to do good works, which God prepared in advance for us to do" (Eph. 2:10 NIV).

And this work—whatever it is—is part of the most significant work one could ever hope to engage in, the reconciliation of the world to Christ Jesus.

You are loved unconditionally and given unparalleled significance by being invited and equipped to participate in God's plan to reconcile the world to Himself. Your emotional needs have been met; you are secure and significant.

This is an incredibly important concept, and to understand why we need to understand the difference between a need and a desire and how we respond when something happens to block either. We easily confuse needs with desires, and doing so can have harmful, if not devastating, consequences for us. Here is why.

When we experience a negative event, our minds immediately classify the event, consciously or subconsciously, as related to a need or desire. If it is related to a need, we feel threatened, damaged, or possibly destroyed. If, on the other hand, we evaluate the event as related to a desire, we feel disappointed, frustrated, or hurt. Do you see the importance of classifying an event correctly?

The same event—a negative one—can result in very different feelings and therefore a very different response from us. We respond very differently when we feel threatened or destroyed than when we feel disappointed or hurt.

Likewise, a positive event goes through the same process. If we evaluate a positive event as related to a need, we feel secure, significant, complete, fulfilled, and content. If we evaluate that event as related to a desire, we feel satisfied. Both evoke positive emotional responses, but the intensity of those responses can be different.

Now there is a big distinction between needs and desires. A need is something we easily develop a dependency on, while a desire can be a one-time event. Here is an example:

If we believe we need our spouse's love, when he or she says, "I love you!" we experience the positive feelings above. But soon afterward, those feelings fade, and we need a new fix. We need our spouse to say it again—soon. Whereas, if our spouse's love is a desire instead of a need, when or if he or she says, "I love you!" we experience satisfaction, with no additional need of a repeat performance by him or her. We just enjoy the moment.

Likewise, when our spouse withholds words or actions of affection—a negative event—and we believe this to be a need, we feel threatened, damaged, incomplete; and we begin to either criticize or elicit affection from him or her to satisfy our need. On the other hand, if we consider our spouse's affection as a desire, we are disappointed when he or she doesn't demonstrate affection toward us, but we aren't damaged or destroyed.

What's my point here? When we realize our needs have been met in Christ—that we are securely loved and have unparalleled significance as we do the work He has prepared for us to do—we discover that nothing can cause us to feel threatened, damaged, or destroyed. Nothing can cause us to develop a dependency for its provision. We can go through life being hurt but not harmed; disappointed but not destroyed or damaged.

When I feel these emotions—threatened, damaged, or ruined—they become red flags to me that I have given something or someone an improper assignment in my life of need versus desire. This person or thing has assumed a role in my life only God should have. And when I put this back in its proper place (related to desire, not need) and make it my deepest conviction that my needs are met in Christ, these things affect me very differently; and out of my fullness, my completeness, my needs met in Christ, I can now minister to those who might have caused my discomfort because I have properly evaluated their action as contributing to a blocked desire, not a need.

Making it your deepest conviction that your needs have been met in Christ is one of the most profound life-changing truths you can ever discover and embrace. It will smooth your ride through life, traveling between satisfaction and disappointment instead of dependency and destruction. You need never feel emotionally threatened again, and if you do, consider the role you have given the event you just experienced. Are you giving this thing or person too much power in your life, making him, her, or it a need versus a desire?

Here are some examples of this megatheme in action:

Job could never have endured his suffering if he'd thought of his family, health, and prosperity as needs. Because they were desires, he wasn't "destroyed"; he was able to say, "Yet though He slay me, I will trust Him" (Job 13:15 NIV)! With his needs met in God, he could suffer great disappointment and remain faithful.

Joseph could never have survived as a slave in Potiphar's household or as a prisoner if he'd viewed his freedom as a need. Instead, when he met his brothers, who were responsible for his slavery and imprisonment, he was able to say, "You intended to harm me, but God intended it for good" (Gen 50:20 NIV). Joseph looked to God alone to meet his needs.

Hosea could never have endured the repeated infidelity of Gomer if he had believed he needed a faithful wife. Instead, because he put his trust in God alone for his needs, Gomer's unfaithfulness, though a great disappointment, didn't threaten or destroy him. He was able to become her savior and redeemer, giving us a great life picture of Christ to come.

Jesus could never have endured the cross and all the suffering leading up to His being fixed on it if He hadn't believed His Father met his needs. Consider this statement: "When they hurled their insults at him, he did not retaliate; when he suffered, he made no threats. Instead, he entrusted himself to him who judges justly" (1 Peter 2:23 NIV).

Jesus didn't take His significance—His security—from the culture, His friends, the people, or His accomplishments. He "entrusted Himself to Him who judges justly." Jesus's Father said several times, "This is My Son in Whom I am well pleased!" That is where Jesus's needs for significance and security were met: in His Father's approval. And we have that same approval when we become sons and daughters of God by accepting the finished work of Jesus on the cross as all sufficient for our sin debt.

"Having been justified by his grace, we might become heirs

having the hope of eternal life" (Titus 3:7 NIV). We become justified, declared not guilty or exonerated when we accept the grace that is ours through Christ Jesus. We then have the approval of the Father as "heirs having the hope of eternal life." Our needs for security and significance have been met though Jesus Christ.

Lastly, recognizing that our needs are met brings great freedom. One day after I was faced with these truths and embraced the truth that my needs are met in Christ, my wife asked me, "Do you need me?"

Now this was a very tough moment, because I love her dearly, and I truly can't imagine life without her. I was very tempted to say—with conviction—that I did need her. But this wasn't really the truth, and the truth actually set us both free.

I said to her, "Dear, you know that you are my only love, the dearest person on earth to me, and I cannot imagine my life without you." Now came a long pause and a deep breath. "But ... I don't need you, and that is very good news to you. You see, you don't have to perform to some standard so that you meet my needs. You can be yourself, and when you do things that are positive, I will feel satisfied; and when you do something hurtful, I will feel disappointed. But nothing you do can ever damage or destroy me; therefore, I can love you with abandon, regardless of your performance or actions toward me."

Having our deepest conviction that our needs are met in Christ frees us to let others be themselves, do whatever they do, and still receive our love in return. Yes, with this conviction, you can truly love those who hurt you and disappoint you; in fact, your greatest opportunity for ministry will be to the ones who hurt you the most. And with needs met in Christ as your deepest conviction, you will be able to be God's instrument of grace to them.

I want to credit Larry Crabb, author of *The Marriage Builder*, for many of these thoughts. I found his book life changing and a great exposition on one of the Bible's great megathemes: our significance and security in God alone.

MEGATHEME 17:

GOD WILL PROVIDE FOR WHAT HE HAS PLANNED

This may be one of the strongest megathemes of scripture and the one God's people least believe or practice. We believe this is true until our resources begin to run short; then anxiety (lack of belief) sets in.

First, let's look at some scriptures that support this megatheme.

> Look at the birds of the air; they do not sow or reap or store away in barns, and yet your heavenly Father feeds them. Are you not much more valuable than they? (Matt. 6:26 NIV)

> Fear the Lord, you his saints,
> for those who fear him lack nothing.
> The lions may grow weak and hungry,
> but those who seek the Lord lack no good thing.
> (Ps. 34:9–10 NIV)

> O Lord our God, as for all this abundance that we have provided for building you a temple for your Holy Name, it comes from your hand, and all of it belongs to you. (1 Chron. 29:16 NIV)

> And my God will meet all your needs according to his glorious riches in Christ Jesus. (Phil. 4:19 NIV)

> He said, "Throw your net on the right side of the boat and you will find some." When they did, they were unable to haul the net in because of the large number of fish. (John 21:6 NIV)

These are just a few of the many passages that speak to God's ability and desire to provide what we need. Clearly, when God gives us an assignment, He will meet any needs we have to carry out that assignment.

Moses saw the deliverance of Israel from the hands of Pharaoh; this was a formidable task. But God gave him all he needed to bring them out of Egypt and provide for them for forty years in the desert until they began their conquest of Canaan.

Ruth the Moabitess left her homeland to return to her mother-in-law's homeland as a widow with no means of support. God provided for her by giving Boaz a generous spirit toward her and allowing her to stay close behind the field workers so she could glean the wheat and barley harvest, picking up food that was intentionally left for her. Then God moved Boaz's heart to be her kinsman-redeemer and give her position and status in the land, ultimately including her in the lineage of Christ.

God commissioned David to commission Solomon to build a temple. God brought all the materials, craftsmen, and laborers to do this work. And He moved the people's hearts to respond generously with their finest possessions. "The people rejoiced at the willing response of their leaders, for they had given freely and wholeheartedly to the Lord. David the king also rejoiced greatly" (1 Chron. 29:9 NIV).

And then there was Elijah; he obeyed the word of the Lord to begin his ministry. "Then the word of the Lord came to Elijah: 'Leave here, turn eastward and hide in the Kerith Ravine, east of the Jordan. You will drink from the brook, and I have ordered the ravens to feed you there'" (1 Kings 17:2–6 NIV).

So he did what the Lord had told him. He went to the Kerith Ravine, east of the Jordan, and stayed there. The ravens brought him bread and meat in the morning, and bread and meat in the evening. He also drank from the brook. So he did what the Lord told him, and God provided for his needs.

Elisha learned from his mentor, but this time he had the faith to believe God would provide for another's need; this was the widow who was about to have her sons taken into slavery to pay her husband's debts. She had nothing but a little oil. Elisha had her borrow all her neighbor's empty jars and pour the oil she had left into all the jars. It must have sounded ridiculous to the widow, but she obeyed—and she was able to take all the jars, sell the oil, and pay her debts.

I could continue with many more examples, such as how God provided Nehemiah with all he needed to rebuild the wall in Jerusalem; or how Zerubbabel was provided with all he needed to rebuild the temple. And angels attended to Jesus in the desert. Then Jesus sent out the "twelve" (Matt. 10) and the "seventy-two" (Luke 10), giving them similar instructions to "not take anything with them" and "stay with whoever offers hospitality." They obeyed, their needs were provided for, and they took the kingdom's light to dark places.

> They went out and preached that people should repent. They drove out many demons and anointed many sick people with oil and healed them. (Mark 6:12–13 NIV)

> The seventy-two returned with joy and said, "Lord, even the demons submit to us in your name." (Luke 10:17 NIV)

We read these accounts, and it is easy to think: *But that was Moses, Ruth, David, Solomon, Elijah, Elisha, Nehemiah, Zerubbabel, Jesus, the apostles, and people Jesus directly empowered (the seventy-two). But He doesn't do that for someone like me, right?*

Here is one of my favorite passages: "And God is able to make all grace abound to you, so that in all things at all times, having all that you need, you will abound in every good work" (2 Cor. 9:8 NIV).

This passage is to you and me, and I have learned that when we obey and trust a passage of scripture, God will give us greater revelation into the depths of that passage's meaning and provision for us. Perhaps a brief personal example would be helpful here.

In 2007, my wife, Ann, and I lived in Mechanicsburg, Pennsylvania, in our home of twenty years, where we raised three children. In February of that year, my boss (Mike Kucek) called me in his office and said God had given him a passage of scripture for me. It was Deuteronomy 28:7–8. "I will bless you in the land that I am giving you."

I had no idea at the time what this meant. What was the "land" God was giving me?

Ann and I had purchased a second home in Annapolis, Maryland, one block from the US Naval Academy (USNA) because we had a son and daughter attending the academy. Our plan was to use the house for a few years and sell it after our children had graduated from USNA.

In the summer of 2007, I attended the Ravi Zacharias International Ministries (RZIM) summer school at the Oxford Center for Christian Apologetics (OCCA) in Oxford, England. There I met Dr. Tom Tarrants, president of the C. S. Lewis Institute. Tom asked senior fellow and Christian apologist Dr. Art Lindsley to mentor and disciple me.

I began a crash-reading course, reading a book each week for two years. Art and I met monthly, and my relationship with the C. S. Lewis Institute and staff matured.

My business began moving from Pennsylvania into Washington, DC, due to new growth and accounts. I was spending two to three days a week in DC, staying in our Annapolis home for convenience; and when the weekend came, Ann said to me, "Can we go to Annapolis for the weekend?" Are you seeing God's handiwork yet?

In May 2008, I suggested to Ann that God may be moving us to Annapolis. She said to me, "Can you look me in the eye and tell me, 'God wants us to move'?"

I couldn't—at least not yet—and she said, "You know what Henry Blackaby (author of *Experiencing God*) says. 'Until God tells you to do something else, keep doing what He last told you to do.'" That morning I headed to Dulles, Virginia, for a business luncheon (a two-hour drive from Mechanicsburg, Pennsylvania). Ten minutes from my destination, my customer called and postponed our luncheon to a later date. Wanting to redeem the trip and my time, I remembered that on that day, the large account I was to visit held their monthly Christian fellowship luncheon, and they offered a five-dollar bag lunch and a guest speaker. I decided to go.

When I arrived and paid for my lunch, I asked who the speaker was that day. The answer? Dr. Henry Blackaby. I took a seat about five rows back from the podium. I loved to read Dr. Blackaby's books, but I had never heard him speak; and the fact that this was the second time on the same morning that his name had been spoken was intriguing. My spiritual antennae were up. By the way, Dr. Tom Tarrants from the C. S. Lewis Institute was also at the event.

Have you ever been at an event where the speaker to make a point will pick someone out of the crowd, someone he or she probably doesn't know, and point at the person as he or she speaks? Dr. Blackaby had my attention with every word, and he was talking about how God has called each of us to be His ambassadors, His watchmen. And at that moment, he turned to me, pointed directly at me (remember, I was only five rows back), and said, "God has called you to be a spiritual watchman on the walls of this nation, especially here in DC" (Isa 62:6; Ezek. 33:7).

I packed my unfinished sandwich in my bag, left the meeting, and drove home to Pennsylvania. Waiting until just the right moment, I said to Ann, "Babe, do you remember our discussion from this morning?"

"You mean about moving to Annapolis?"

"Yes."

She asked, "Remember what Henry Blackaby said?"

I answered, "Henry Blackaby told me!"

After giving her the details and seeing the conviction in my spirit that I had heard from Jesus, she said, "I need six months to renovate the house here in Pennsylvania so we can sell it." We spent the next six months preparing the house for sale.

Not doubting the call to Annapolis/DC but still lacking clarity as to why God might be calling us there (to leave the security of Pennsylvania for the unknown of Annapolis), I sought clarity, and God gave it.

Tom Tarrants approached me at this time to consider starting an extension of the C. S. Lewis Institute (CSLI) in Annapolis so people there could participate in the discipleship programs CSLI offered without having to commute to DC.

About the same time, walking back from the local coffee shop to the Annapolis house (still our second home), I stopped at the corner in front of the house. Suddenly, I saw it. Our house was one block from the US Naval Academy, two blocks from Saint John's College, one block from the state capitol, and one block from the downtown Annapolis community. God had strategically placed this home at this place and for this time so He could advance His reign over this community (the "land").

Art Lindsley confirmed this one evening when he stayed at the house and was made acutely aware of the convergence of community, government, military, and education at this geographic location and its accompanying spiritual warfare.

Furthermore, on November 12, 2008, I read the book *DAWS*, given to me by another spiritual mentor, John Bishop, about the life of Dawson Troutman, founder of the Navigators. I read how Isaiah 60:11 had been instrumental in shaping his call to found the Navigators.

> Your gates will always stand open,
> they will never be shut, day or night,
> so that men may bring you the wealth of the nations—
> their kings led in triumphal procession.
> (Isa. 60:11 NIV)

The meaning of this was clear to me. Ann and I were to be stewards of the Annapolis house and make it available to all who came because God would bring people to this house and the institute who were going to be significant in His kingdom. Future kings will pass through, people who will be the "wealth of the nations," bringing light, hope, and salvation to the people of the nations.

In January 2009, we started the CSLI Annapolis extension. Ann named the house in Annapolis "The Aslan House" (after the Christ figure in C. S. Lewis's Narnia books). We put our house in Pennsylvania on the market (it sold in a week) and made "The Aslan House" our home.

Also at this time, I had just read *The Autobiography of George*

Mueller, the account of how he trusted God for the funds and resources to support his calling to build orphanages in the United Kingdom in the early 1900s. One statement he made struck me just as Isaiah 60:11 had: "I want this ministry to give evidence to the fact that there is reality in dealing with God alone!"

I'm not saying all fund-raising and ministry operations should function this way, but God was clearly saying to me that I should completely rely on Him for every resource I needed to do the work of the institute. That included funds, mentors, fellows, speakers, venues, and so forth.

Eight years later, God has provided all I have needed year to year to conduct the operations of the institute without having to fund-raise, recruit, or sell the institute. God has asked me to let people know what He has asked me to do, invite them to participate, and leave the results and resources to Him.

Again, I'm not saying this is the model for everyone, but it is the model God gave me to follow, and He has proved faithful in that the C. S. Lewis Institute-Annapolis has had "all grace available to us, so that in all things, at all times, having all that we needed, we have been able to abound in every good work" (2 Cor. 9:8 NIV). Praise be to God!

After trusting God for finances and resources, He surrounded me with godly men to oversee the plans and activities of CSLI Annapolis (Jim Hiskey, John Bishop, George Anderson, Sig Berg, and later Alan "Blues" Baker). The first fellows program launched in June 2009, and we have had over 125 fellows graduate from the Annapolis Institute since then as well as opportunities to start discipleship programs in the community (fellows) and in education (college students). We also offer ministries to area pastors and state legislators.

Whatever God may be calling you to do, He will be faithful to you, since He has been faithful to countless other servants, to provide all you will need to accomplish His purposes. God will provide for what He has planned.

A FOLLOWER OF JESUS WILL FACE ADVERSITY

This final chapter offers four megathemes for the mature disciple of Jesus. They address the certainty of adversity, the need to persevere, the expectation of limited insight from God on the nature of our adversity, and the hope that God gives us that He will redeem every bad story in our lives for His glory and our good.

MEGATHEME 18:

IF YOU ARE LIVING IN OBEDIENCE, YOU WILL FACE ADVERSITY

If I were to make a list of the "top ten lies of Satan," in one of the top spots would be this: "If you are a follower of Jesus, it should go well for you and your family."

I have met many followers of Jesus who seem confused, even angry, that since they became a follower of Jesus, they have had trials and adversity.

What this really reflects is a wrong understanding of God, grace, and our salvation. We have a deeply rooted assumption that if we do what we should be doing (the teachings of scripture), God will do what He should be doing (taking care of us and our family). We have entered a contractual or transactional relationship with God.

But God doesn't deal with us that way. We earlier discussed that holiness, not happiness, is God's priority for us. We also discussed the fact that the desert is often God's furnace to purify us or make us holy. But now I want to get more specific and suggest that we should not only expect adversity when we become followers of Jesus but also welcome it when it comes.

Adversity is a sure sign that we are

1. true children of God; and
2. His soldiers "effectively" engaged in battle.

Here are a few passages of scripture to show us that enduring hardship should be expected of a disciple of Jesus, a child of God:

> Surely you remember, brothers, our toil and hardship; we worked night and day in order not to be a burden to anyone while we preached the Gospel of God to you. (1 Thess. 2:9 NIV)

> But you, keep your head in all situations, endure hardship, do the work of an evangelist, discharge all the duties of your ministry. (2 Tim. 4:5 NIV)

> Endure hardship as discipline; God is treating you as sons. For what son is not disciplined by his father? (Heb. 12:7 NIV)

Also consider Paul's second letter to the Corinthians, in which he shared his persecutions and hardships for the sake of Christ.

> Are they servants of Christ? (I am out of my mind to talk like this.) I am more. I have worked much harder, been in prison more frequently, been flogged more severely, and been exposed to death again and again. Five times I received from the Jews the forty lashes minus one. Three times I was beaten with rods, once I was stoned,

three times I was shipwrecked, I spent a night and a day in the open sea, I have been constantly on the move. I have been in danger from rivers, in danger from bandits, in danger from my own countrymen, in danger from Gentiles; in danger in the city, in danger in the country, in danger at sea; and in danger from false brothers. I have labored and toiled and have often gone without sleep; I have known hunger and thirst and have often gone without food; I have been cold and naked. Besides everything else, I face daily the pressure of my concern for all the churches. (2 Cor. 11:23–28 NIV)

Surely, if Paul suffered hardship for the sake of Jesus, shouldn't we expect it? And hardship is also a sign of us being effective soldiers. Paul considered himself a soldier when he stated the following to the Philippians and Philemon:

But I think it is necessary to send back to you Epaphroditus, my brother, fellow worker and fellow soldier, who is also your messenger, whom you sent to take care of my needs. (Phil. 2:25 NIV)

To Apphia our sister, to Archippus our fellow soldier and to the church that meets in your home. (Philem. 1:2 NIV)

And specifically to Timothy, he associated hardship with being a good soldier. "Endure hardship with us like a good soldier of Christ Jesus" (2 Tim. 2:3 NIV).

The Bible is replete with examples of hardship accompanying effective soldiers of God.

- All but one of the apostles were martyred.
- Most of the prophets were persecuted or killed.

- Stephen was martyred.
- Nero fed countless numbers of early Christians to the lions.
- Job suffered terribly.
- Daniel was thrown into a lions' den.
- The three Hebrew children were thrown into the fiery furnace.

What biblical basis do we have for expecting things to go well for us when we become followers of Jesus? But I said earlier that we should actually welcome hardship when it comes. Doesn't that seem counterintuitive, perhaps even masochistic?

Now we come to the heart of this megatheme. For what or whom do you really live? What is the supreme desire of your heart? When you read this passage, what do you think about?

> Delight yourself in the Lord
> and he will give you the desires of your heart.
> (Ps. 37:4 NIV)

What is the desire of your heart? If your desire involves a long life free of pain and suffering, you won't be tracking with this megatheme at this moment. Welcoming trials, persecutions, discipline, and hardship will be difficult for you to comprehend. Please hang in there; what happens in the next few sentences could be life changing for you.

I want to share with you a prayer the Lord gave me many years back when I was struggling with the passage above (Ps. 37:4). I was trying to be the best follower of Jesus I could, and I had difficulty in my life that was crippling me. How could this passage be true? I didn't believe I was receiving the desires of my heart. Here is the prayer the Lord gave me:

> Lord, today make me more like your Son (Rom. 8:29).
>
> I will look to You and You alone for my honor (significance) and my future (security) (Ps. 62:7).

137

My heart's desire, my only desire, is to please You; Your approval is all I desire (1 Peter 2:23; 2 Peter 1:17).

My life's goal is to fulfill Your purpose, Your plan for my life (Eph. 2:10).

I will do anything You ask, NO EXCEPTIONS, and leave the consequences and my defense to You (Job 13:15).

Amen (let it be so)!

Let's dissect this prayer sentence by sentence. First is "Today, make me more like your Son (Rom. 8:29)."

Do you remember what God's Son did out of love for us and His Father?

And being found in appearance as a man,
he humbled himself
and became obedient to death—
even death on a cross!
(Phil. 2:8 NIV)

The Father asked His Son to go to a cross; this was an act of love for us and His Father. I am saying when I pray this line, "Father, today, make me like Your Son—willing to suffer any adversity, trusting that You will bring the greatest good for the greatest number and for the longest period of time—and help me to do this with joy."

Joy—really? Stay with me.

Second line: "I will look to You and You alone for my honor (significance) and my future (security) (Ps. 62:7)."

Remember the questions "For what or for whom do you really live? What is the supreme desire of your heart?"

Who are you trying to please? If it is your deepest conviction that at the end of time the only opinion of you that will matter is God's opinion, does it not make sense that you should be trying to please God and God alone?

My honor, my salvation, and my future depend on God and God alone. At the end of the day, the greatest reward I can ever receive is the clapping of two nail-scarred hands.

This now leads to the third line: "My heart's desire, my only desire, is to please You; Your approval is all I desire (2 Peter 1:17; 1 Peter 2:23)."

The first two lines take my thinking from earthly, carnal thinking to kingdom thinking. At the end of the day, all I want is to hear God say to me, "Well done, good and faithful servant!" If my mind has now given assent to this truth, I am ready to move to the fourth line: "My life's goal is to fulfill Your purpose, Your plan for my life (Eph. 2:10)."

I want to fulfill God's plan for my life. I believe with all my heart that His plan will result in my greatest satisfaction and significance. No other plan allows me to be more consequential in His kingdom. Any other plan will only diminish my effectiveness in God's plan to reconcile the world to Himself and bring "sons and daughters of Satan" (John 8:44) to become "adopted children of God" (Eph. 1:5).

Now that my thoughts are aligned, the ultimate goal of my life is to "delight myself in the Lord," and by doing this I now willingly align my desires to be those that meet His approval and accomplish His plan for my life. And I am ready to pray the last line of the prayer with conviction. "I will do anything You ask, NO EXCEPTIONS, and leave the consequences and my defense to You (Job 13:15)."

I now welcome whatever God asks me to do, because I only want to please Him. I trust that what He asks me to do will result in great good in the kingdom, and I trust Him with the consequences of whatever He asks me to do. No exceptions!

I know I won't be abandoned in whatever He asks of me. "Who shall separate us from the love of Christ? Shall trouble or hardship or persecution or famine or nakedness or danger or sword?" (Rom. 8:35 NIV).

And I can embrace whatever He asks me to do, whatever hardship comes, with joy. Remember, joy doesn't mean happy feelings. Joy is that deep-seated conviction that all is well, that these difficult circumstances have great purpose, that rather than being a victim, I have been chosen to endure these hardships.

Jesus had this perspective, and He was able to endure what the Father had asked of Him with joy. "Let us fix our eyes on Jesus, the author and perfecter of our faith, who for the joy set before him endured the cross, scorning its shame, and sat down at the right hand of the throne of God" (Heb. 12:2 NIV).

Jesus didn't enjoy the suffering of the cross, but He did endure that suffering "for the joy set before Him," trusting that the Father was going to bring about great good through His obedience.

When I pray the last line of the prayer above, I admit I sometimes clench my teeth and grip the chair before me because I don't know what I might be asking or inviting God to do with my life. It may be as difficult as martyrdom or the endurance of a painful and disabling disease.

Perhaps my deepest conviction is the following:

> My salvation and my honor depend on God;
> God's approval is what I desire most;
> My life's goal, my only goal, is to fulfill God's plan
> for my life.

Then what follows is to ask Him to help me become more like His Son and accept whatever He may bring into my life (no exceptions) with joy, the conviction that it is best for me and for all who are in my sphere of influence and beyond.

It is a lie from the pit of hell that if you become a follower of Jesus, you shouldn't have adversity. That lie will cause you to see yourself as a victim and God as a tyrant when He asks you to do something for His kingdom's sake.

But as a follower of Jesus, you aren't a victim, and God isn't your enemy. You are being developed into the likeness of His Son. You are chosen to accept certain hardships (which He will enable you to bear) because you are uniquely qualified to endure those hardships so that the greatest good can come to the greatest number and for the longest period. If you are living in obedience, you *will* have adversity.

MEGATHEME 19:

WE ARE SAVED BY GRACE, BUT WE MUST PERSEVERE

We have already discussed that there are many "both ands" in scripture. Two truths may appear to be in tension but are true at all times. Any attempt to resolve the tension results in theological error.

One of those truths is that we are saved by grace, but we must persevere.

Nothing in the discussion that follows is meant to diminish the truth that we are saved by grace and—to paraphrase Paul—not by works so that no man can boast. Paul set the foundation for these teachings and never wavered. And scripture is clear that when a person expresses a genuinely repentant faith, salvation comes to that person at that moment; and the Holy Spirit begins the work of conforming that person into the likeness of Christ, which is a lifelong process.

The key phrase above is "genuinely repentant faith." We have already discussed the need for not only faith in Christ but also repentant faith in Christ. Now we add another qualifier: not a work but descriptor of the professed faith—that the profession was an act of the person's will, who sincerely desired to turn from all sin and become a follower, disciple, or learner of Jesus.

Here are some scriptures warning us against an insincere faith versus a genuine, repentant faith:

THE CHILDREN OF ABRAHAM

"To the Jews who had believed him, Jesus said, 'If you hold to my teaching, you are really my disciples'" (John 8:31 NIV). We must hold to Jesus's teachings. Disregarding His teachings repeatedly begs the question of the sincerity of the profession of faith.

Jesus further gave us a picture of those whose professions weren't genuine when He quoted Isaiah. "'These people honor me with their lips, but their hearts are far from me'" (Matt. 15:8 NIV).

John also addressed the insincere follower of Jesus. "They went out from us, but they did not really belong to us. For if they had belonged to us, they would have remained with us; but their going showed that none of them belonged to us" (1 John 2:19 NIV).

Now, just as Paul's teachings best represent the first part of our megatheme—that salvation is by grace alone—James's teachings represent the second portion of the megatheme when he says, "As the body without the spirit is dead, so faith without deeds is dead" (James 2:26 NIV).

If we profess to have faith but never demonstrate that faith by accompanying deeds, our actions beg the question of the genuine nature of our profession. Jesus said it this way: "Remain in me, and I will remain in you. No branch can bear fruit by itself; it must remain in the vine. Neither can you bear fruit unless you remain in me" (John 15:4 NIV).

A true follower of Jesus will bear fruit. What is this fruit? It is the results that could have been accomplished only through the accompanying work of the Spirit in one's life. If your life shows no change or progress toward the likeness of Christ or advancement in the spiritual fruits listed in Galatians 5:22, then it begs the question of your original confession of faith.

This is a passage that should cause every follower of Jesus concern: "Many will say to me on that day, 'Lord, Lord, did we not prophesy in your name, and in your name drive out demons and perform many miracles?' Then I will tell them plainly, 'I never knew you. Away from me, you evildoers!'" (Matt. 7:22–23 NIV). Those were people who thought they were in the kingdom of God. They labored in doing things for God, *but they had no relationship with God*; this fact brings us to a pause.

If you have any questions about the genuine nature of your

faith profession, you can fix that right now before you read another sentence. Now, if something within you just recoiled or drew back—if you felt resentment toward this suggestion—you may be in danger of being one of those whom the passage above addresses. A true follower of Jesus wouldn't hesitate to reaffirm his or her commitment to Christ at this very moment.

I recently stood outside my home when a neighbor came by and asked me about the plaque beside our front door. It says, "Aslan House." After explaining that our house is the home of the C. S. Lewis Institute, where people who want to be better followers of Jesus come to learn more about Jesus's teachings and apply them to their lives, this neighbor said, "Oh, I am just not where I should be on all that. I used to be active in my church; I used to teach my children about God, but I have fallen away from Him in recent years."

I said to my neighbor, "You know that is easily fixed?"

He said, "No. How?"

I said, "We can pray together right now, and you can tell Jesus that you are sorry for ignoring Him and putting so many other things before Him, that you want to recommit your life to His plan and purpose for your life, and that you will go forward from this day on and serve Him with His help." And we prayed that prayer as tears streamed down my neighbor's cheeks.

Now my neighbor needs to go and demonstrate that his confession of faith was genuine. Paul said, "Therefore, my dear friends, as you have always obeyed—not only in my presence, but now much more in my absence—continue to work out your salvation with fear and trembling, for it is God who works in you to will and to act according to his good purpose" (Phil. 2:12–13 NIV).

When Paul said, "Work out," he meant to demonstrate, to show by our actions that our faith is genuine. While our actions don't save us, faith without any follow-up activity is, as James so aptly put it, dead.

Scripture has many examples of people who began well but didn't finish well.

Lot's wife was being rescued from Sodom and Gomorrah, yet she loved the things of her world more than the things of God. She looked back and become a pillar of salt.

The seer Balaam had some conversations with God while trying to find a way to curse the Israelites so he could collect a big reward from their enemies. God kept telling him he couldn't do this. He loved things more than he valued a relationship with God, and ultimately the Israelites killed him when they attacked the Midianites (Num. 31:8).

The Spirit of God came on Saul in power in his early days as king (1 Sam. 11:6). But Saul began to love his kingship more than God, and the Spirit of God departed from him (1 Sam. 16:14). He died with his sons as a defeated king in disgrace, because he didn't persevere in his love and affection for God.

Solomon began his reign this way: "When Solomon finished praying, fire came down from heaven and consumed the burnt offering and the sacrifices, and the glory of the Lord filled the temple. The priests could not enter the temple of the Lord because the glory of the Lord filled it" (2 Chron. 7:1–2 NIV).

The glory of the Lord filled the temple and gave Solomon great wisdom to rule the people. But Solomon ended his life this way: "So Solomon did evil in the eyes of the Lord; he did not follow the Lord completely, as David his father had done. On a hill east of Jerusalem, Solomon built a high place for Chemosh the detestable god of Moab, and for Molech the detestable god of the Ammonites. He did the same for all his foreign wives, who burned incense and offered sacrifices to their gods" (1 Kings 11:6–8 NIV).

Judas walked with Christ and was one of the twelve and seventy-two Jesus sent out to spread the gospel. The report is that these two groups cast out demons in Jesus's name and did many healings. Yet Judas was disappointed that Jesus wasn't focused on establishing an earthly kingdom, so he betrayed Him. Will he be one who says, "Lord, Lord, … did I not …?" on that day and hears Jesus say, "Depart from me, I never knew you"?

Jesus gave us this warning about committing to follow Him and then turning back: "Jesus replied, 'No one who puts his hand to the plow and looks back is fit for service in the kingdom of God'" (Luke 9:62 NIV).

True followers of Jesus will remain committed to the task. They persevere; they finish strong.

Jesus warns us against being lukewarm in our attitude toward Him. "I know your deeds, that you are neither cold nor hot. I wish you were either one or the other! So, because you are lukewarm—neither hot nor cold—I am about to spit you out of my mouth" (Rev. 3:15–17 NIV).

What are the symptoms of lukewarmness?

- What two or three things has God given you as a priority for your life right now?
- When was the last time God used you to bless or pray for a neighbor, coworker, friend, or family member?
- Are you tithing the amount God has put on your heart to give?
- Are you faithful to the gathering of the saints and regularly attending your church and small groups?
- Are you owning the responsibility for the spiritual education of your children, or do you look to the church to do that?
- When was the last time you went to a quiet place and just gave thanks to God for all His blessings toward you?
- When was the last time you meditated on the word and let the Spirit speak to you through its contents?
- Are you confident you are following God's plan for your life right now?

How many of these questions gave you pause? That is, you really don't know the answer, or you know the answer, and it's not pleasing to God. All those questions could indicate either an area of lukewarmness in your life or a lukewarm life. This isn't how God wants you to live your life. He is inviting you to participate with Him in one of the most amazing causes ever: the reconciliation of men and women to Him and to one another. There is no greater joy than to see relationships healed through reconciliation, and that is because these are earthly representations of a greater spiritual event: the return and reconciliation of a prodigal son or daughter to the Father.

God didn't make you so you could make a profession of faith and then go about living your life any way you choose, believing your ticket to eternal life has been punched. In fact, we are warned against this attitude and encouraged to "work out" or "demonstrate" our salvation. Faith without works is dead. Dallas Willard says it best: "Grace is not opposed to effort, it is opposed to earning. Earning is an attitude. Effort is an action. Grace, you know, does not just have to do with forgiveness of sins alone."[5]

We are saved by grace, but we must persevere.

MEGATHEME 20:

THERE ARE SOME THINGS GOD IS NOT GOING TO TELL US ... AND WE SHOULD EXPECT THAT

Why isn't God more forthcoming on information that would help us in our walk with Him? Many times people have asked this question in the scriptures, and I am sure you have asked this more than once in your own walk with Jesus.

I am going to focus on one specific instance in scripture when this question was asked and then pose some thoughts on why God doesn't answer every question with the clarity we think He should.

Habakkuk saw his own land, Judah, in a state of lawlessness and idolatry. The righteous were oppressed (see Hab. 1:4, 13), and the people were living in open sin, worshipping idols (see Hab. 2:18–19). He knew Babylon was gaining power and that God was going to use Nebuchadnezzar to judge Judah. And he asked this question:

> Why do you make me look at injustice?
> Why do you tolerate wrong?
> Destruction and violence are before me;

there is strife, and conflict abounds.
The wicked hem in the righteous,
so that justice is perverted.
(Hab. 1:3–4 NIV)

God answered Habakkuk.

Look at the nations and watch—
and be utterly amazed.
For I am going to do something in your days
that you would not believe,
even if you were told.
I am raising up the Babylonians,
that ruthless and impetuous people,
who sweep across the whole earth
to seize dwelling places not their own.
(Hab. 1:5–6 NIV)

Habakkuk clarified his question in verses 12–13.

O Lord, you have appointed them (Babylon) to execute
judgment;
O Rock, you have ordained them to punish.
Why then do you tolerate the treacherous?
Why are you silent while the wicked
swallow up those more righteous than themselves?
(Hab. 1:12–13 NIV)

It is a variation of an age-old question: Why do the wicked seem
to prosper? But Habakkuk added this to the question: Why do You
allow the wicked to swallow up those more righteous? That is, as
bad as Judah has become, is it right to allow a more wicked nation
to judge her?

The Lord answered further in Habakkuk 2:2–10. He agreed that
the Babylonians were wicked but declared that they would destroy

themselves in the end through their own pride and wickedness. He also said this "revelation awaits an appointed time" (Hab. 2:3).

Habakkuk was left to trust that God knew what He was doing, and while it didn't look just for God to use Babylon to punish Judah, God's plan would in the end prove right.

And this theme is repeated in scripture. Why isn't God more forthcoming in His plans for us and the world? I want to propose a thought:

We have an enemy (Satan). He is intelligent, powerful, crafty, and always at work to thwart God's plans; but he is not omniscient. He needs information so he can use it against God and His people.

The Old Testament (OT) pointed to Jesus and how He would come and what He would do. Yet in the first century AD, the Jews still didn't recognize Him because God had left enough information out that only those with additional information (such as the disciples) knew Him for sure. Why?

Satan used the information he had to try to thwart God's plan. Through Herod, he killed babies in Bethlehem; he tempted Christ in person. Through Peter he tried to keep Him from going to Jerusalem, and ultimately he had Him crucified (through the high priests, Judas, Pilate, and the crowds of people). Not being able to thwart Christ's entry and works in the world, he thought he could ultimately win by taking His life and making Him suffer a humiliating death on a cross.

There was information in the OT that became clear *after* the crucifixion that this was Christ's mission in the world, but that information didn't lead anyone to know this to be true *before* the crucifixion (even the disciples). Thus, the enemy didn't know it either and was unable to stop God's plan.

We understand the book of Daniel and Revelation the same way the first-century Jews understood the OT prophecies about Christ. There was enough information there so that when and after the events happened, people recognized prophecy was being fulfilled; but there was enough left out so the enemy would be unsuccessful in his attempts to block God's plan.

God did this on a personal level as well. He withheld specific information from us for many reasons:

- We may not be able to receive that information now; it could cause us grief and anxiety we don't need to or couldn't suffer in the present.
- Our enemy can use that information to try to prevent the events from happening and cause us unnecessary pain and suffering, denying us the good God intended for us.

There are some things God isn't going to tell us, and we should expect and accept that fact.

MEGATHEME 21:

GOD'S WAY OF REDEEMING A BAD STORY IS TO WRAP IT IN A BETTER ONE, A EUCATASTROPHE

This is the promise to all followers of Jesus we find in Romans 8:28. "And we know that in all things God works for the good of those who love him, who have been called according to his purpose" (Rom. 8:28 NIV).

Eucatastrophe is a term credited to J. R. R. Tolkien. It is formed by affixing the Greek prefix *eu*, meaning "good," to *catastrophe*, meaning "overturning" or "a sudden turn" (hence, a "turn for the good").

In a eucatastrophe, a great evil is overcome by a greater good, resulting in a good conclusion, and we love those kinds of stories. Think of some of your favorite children stories, novels, movies, or real-life experiences, and you will find eucatastrophe. My wife and I enjoy watching the Hallmark Channel. Every one of those stores is predictable. Boy meets girl, and they fall in love. Something bad happens, and all looks lost. Then something amazingly good happens; they are reconciled, and they live happily ever after. It is so predictable, but it is a eucatastrophe, and we love it.

I think of the children's fairy tale "Snow White." How boring would this story be without the poisoned apple? But because of the poisoned apple, Snow White meets her prince and lives happily ever after.

Why do we love stories that involve a greater good overcoming a great evil? Tolkien said this is because those stories represent what Christ did for us. The crucifixion was the worst thing that ever happened to mankind, and the resurrection was the eucatastrophe or the best thing that ever happened. Tolkien further suggested that we are wired to appreciate the gospel; therefore, any story that bears a resemblance to it (eucatastrophe) will resonate with us.[6]

This principle that God redeems a bad story by wrapping it in a better one (eucatastrophe) is a megatheme, because it is present throughout the stories of scripture.

Adam and Eve had everything in the garden, but they disobeyed God's instructions and ate the forbidden fruit. They became separated from God and ashamed, and they ran from Him, but He went to them, clothed them with animal skins, and gave them a promise of redemption to come. That is a eucatastrophe.

Joseph was the firstborn from his father's favorite wife. He was the apple of his father's eye. His brothers despised him and sold him into slavery. His master's wife falsely accused him of sexual impropriety. He was thrown into prison and miraculously brought into the presence of Pharaoh, where he was promoted to become prime minister of Egypt.

Moses had everything in Pharaoh's palace; he was destined for royalty. He began to identify with his people, the Israelites, and ended up murdering an Egyptian and fleeing Egypt to the desert. There in the desert he learned how to be a shepherd. He gave up any notions of greatness and met God in a divine encounter. He was then empowered to be the deliverer of the Israelites.

God gave Samson a great gift of strength, which he used to deliver Israel from their enemies, the Philistines. He was betrayed by a friend and fell into the hands of his enemy, where he was tortured and blinded. But God strengthened him and placed him in a strategic location to destroy his enemies, and "he killed many more when he died than while he lived" (Judg. 16:30). This tragic story is wrapped in a better one. Samson was given the opportunity to be a type of Christ—and this is a eucatastrophe.

Esther, a woman of great beauty, was taken from her home, made to participate in a beauty pageant for a pagan king, and taken into his house as part of his harem. Then she was made queen. If the story ended here, it wouldn't be a happy one. I'm not sure it was Esther's dream to be in the harem of a pagan king, even as queen. She was a Hebrew, and because she was raised by a devout Hebrew—Mordecai—she no doubt had been raised to know the importance of marrying a Hebrew man, and she hoped and planned to do this. But the story didn't end there. God uniquely positioned her to be the person who could intercede for her people at the risk of her life; she kept them from being exterminated at the hand of a wicked man named Haman. She did intercede, and her people were saved. Then she realized God had put her in this position for "such a time as this" (Est. 4:14).

Hosea married a woman he loved greatly, but she was unfaithful to him. He spent many years being faithful to her and raising her children—not all of whom were his—and ultimately purchased her when she was sold on a slave block. We get this beautiful picture of reconciliation and redemption. Hosea 3:3 (NIV) says, "Then I told her, 'You are to live with me many days; you must not be a prostitute or be intimate with any man, and I will live with you.'"

Hosea's dream marriage became a nightmare and then was restored to him but with much, much more. God used Hosea's circumstances to give us a life picture of our waywardness from Him and how He was going to come and redeem us from our slavery to sin and live with us forever. Hosea was a type of Christ to come. His bad story had become a preview of the greatest story ever told—a eucatastrophe.

Joseph was engaged to the girl of his dreams and then discovered she was pregnant. After he experienced much emotional anguish and decided to quietly divorce her, an angel of the Lord visited him and told him about the special circumstances of Mary's pregnancy. He decided to shoulder her circumstances, endure any ridicule or shame the community might try to lay on him for her condition, and be her husband and protector. He then became the earthly father of God, the Savior of the world.

God redeems a bad story by wrapping it in a better one, and this is a eucatastrophe.

We are all living eucatastrophes; none of us were born perfect, none are living perfect lives, and none of us are experiencing a blissful existence. All of us were born broken, we are self-centered, and we have been hurt by others—and we hurt others. But God is at work in our lives and the lives of those we have hurt to redeem our bad stories with a better one if we allow Him to do so.

What is your "poisoned apple?"

Complete this statement: I am grateful to God for everything in my life except _____. This is very likely the poisoned apple in your life. It need not destroy you, diminish you, incapacitate you, or ruin your life.

Let's go back to the story of Snow White. What would she say now if we were to ask her this question? "Snow White, what do you think about that poisoned apple?"

She would likely respond, "It was a bummer! It was painful and emotionally hurtful to be betrayed by someone who was supposed to be my guardian, and it almost killed me; *but* because of the poison apple, I met my husband, the prince, and because of that I am grateful for the apple."

You will know when God has accomplished His purpose for allowing the poisoned apple in your life; you will come to be grateful for the poisoned apple. Being grateful doesn't deny the pain of the loss or injury from the apple, but it acknowledges the good God has done and is doing in your life as a result.

God wants to redeem your poisoned apple and replace your bad story with a greater one—a story involving a Prince—so your life's story becomes a eucatastrophe.

No one desires a poisoned apple, but God can bring such good from it that you can look back and say, "If the only way I could have had the relationship with God that I have now was through the poisoned apple, then I'm grateful God allowed it in my life."

As I once heard Ravi Zacharias say, "Never confuse pain and suffering as a lack of God's blessing in your life; for through pain and suffering we come to know God better, and that is the greatest blessing of all." "Give thanks in all circumstances, for this is God's will for you in Christ Jesus" (1 Thess. 5:18 NIV).

God's way of redeeming a bad story is to wrap it in a better one—a eucatastrophe.

APPENDIX A

HOW ACCURATE IS THE BIBLE?

by Ken Boa

"Jack, you're always quoting the Bible to me as if were the last word on issues about life. How can you base your life on a book that's so full of contradictions and errors? Historians and scientists have long since proven that the Bible is inaccurate and unreliable."

Many people are of the opinion that the teachings of the Bible are outdated, contradictory, and full of scientific and historical errors. With few exceptions, they have reached these conclusions through second- and third-hand sources rather than from their own study of the Bible.

Consider the following statements:

- The Bible says God helps those who help themselves.
- The books of the New Testament were written centuries after the events they describe.
- "Cleanliness is next to godliness" is in the Bible.
- According to the Bible, the earth is flat.
- The earliest New Testament manuscripts go back only to the fourth or fifth centuries AD.
- The Bible teaches that the earth is the center of the universe.
- The English Bible is a translation of a translation of a translation (and so forth) of the original, and fresh errors were introduced in each stage of the process.

How many of these statements do you think are true? The answer is that all of them are false. Yet these false impressions persist in the minds of many, and misinformation like this produces a skeptical attitude toward the Bible.

In this booklet, we will consider a number of objections to the accuracy and reliability of the Bible to help you make a more informed decision as to whether it is authoritative.

"How can you be sure that the Bible is the same now as when it was written? The Bible has been copied and translated so many times! Haven't you ever played the game where people sit in a circle and pass a sentence from one person to the next until it comes back around in a completely distorted version? If that could happen in a room in just a few minutes, think of all the errors and changes that must have filled the Bible in the centuries since it was first written!"

There are three lines of evidence that support the claim that the biblical documents are reliable: these are the bibliographic test, the internal test, and the external test. The first test examines the biblical manuscripts, the second test deals with the claims made by the biblical authors, and the third test looks to outside confirmation of the biblical content.

I. THE BIBLIOGRAPHIC TEST

A. The Quantity of Manuscripts

In the case of the Old Testament, there are a small number of Hebrew manuscripts, because the Jewish scribes ceremonially buried imperfect and worn manuscripts. Many ancient manuscripts were also lost or destroyed during Israel's turbulent history. Also, the Old Testament text was standardized by the Masoretic Jews by the sixth century AD, and all manuscripts that deviated from the Masoretic Text were evidently eliminated. But the existing Hebrew manuscripts are supplemented by the Dead Sea Scrolls, the Septuagint (a third-century BC Greek translation of the Old Testament), the Samaritan

Pentateuch, and the Targums (ancient paraphrases of the Old Testament), as well as the Talmud (teachings and commentaries related to the Hebrew scriptures).

The quantity of New Testament manuscripts is unparalleled in ancient literature. There are over five thousand Greek manuscripts, about eight thousand Latin manuscripts, and another one thousand manuscripts in other languages (Syriac, Coptic, and so forth). In addition to this extraordinary number, there are tens of thousands of citations of New Testament passages by the early church fathers. In contrast, the typical number of existing manuscript copies for any of the works of the Greek and Latin authors, such as Plato, Aristotle, Caesar, or Tacitus, ranges from one to twenty.

B. The Quality of Manuscripts

Because of the great reverence the Jewish scribes held toward the scriptures, they exercised extreme care in making new copies of the Hebrew Bible. The entire scribal process was specified in meticulous detail to minimize the possibility of even the slightest error. The number of letters, words, and lines were counted, and the middle letters of the Pentateuch and the Old Testament were determined. If a single mistake was discovered, the entire manuscript would be destroyed.

Because of this extreme care, the quality of the manuscripts of the Hebrew Bible surpasses all other ancient manuscripts. The 1947 discovery of the Dead Sea Scrolls provided a significant check on this, because these Hebrew scrolls antedate the earliest Masoretic Old Testament manuscripts by about one thousand years. But in spite of this time span, the number of variant readings between the Dead Sea Scrolls and the Masoretic Text is quite small, and most of these are variations in spelling and style.

While the quality of the Old Testament manuscripts is excellent, that of the New Testament is very good—considerably better than the manuscript quality of other ancient documents. Because of the thousands of New Testament manuscripts, there are many variant readings, but these variants are actually used by scholars to reconstruct the original readings by determining which variant best explains the others in any given passage. Some of these variant readings crept into the manuscripts because of visual errors in copying or because of auditory errors when a group of scribes copied manuscripts that were read aloud. Other errors resulted from faulty writing, memory, and judgment, and still others from well-meaning scribes who thought they were correcting the text. Nevertheless, only a small number of these differences affect the sense of the passages, and only a fraction of these have any real consequences. Furthermore, no variant readings are significant enough to call into question any of the doctrines of the New Testament. The New Testament can be regarded as 99.5 percent pure, and the correct readings for the remaining 0.5 percent can often be ascertained with a fair degree of probability by the practice of textual criticism.

C. The Time Span of Manuscripts

Apart from some fragments, the earliest Masoretic manuscript of the Old Testament is dated at AD 895. This is due to the systematic destruction of worn manuscripts by the Masoretic scribes. However, the discovery of the Dead Sea Scrolls dating from 200 BC to AD 68 drastically reduced the time span from the writing of the Old Testament books to our earliest copies of them.

The time span of the New Testament manuscripts is exceptional. The manuscripts written on papyrus came from the second and third centuries AD. The John Rylands Fragment (P52) of the Gospel of John is dated at AD 117–38, only a few decades after the Gospel was written. The Bodmer Papyri are dated from AD 175–225, and the Chester Beatty Papyri date from about AD 250. The time span for most of the New Testament is less than two hundred years (and some books are within one hundred years) from the date of authorship to the date of our earliest manuscripts. This can be sharply contrasted with the average gap of over one thousand years between the composition and the earliest copy of the writings of other ancient authors.

To summarize the bibliographic test, the Old and New Testaments enjoy far greater manuscript attestation in terms of quantity, quality, and time span than any other ancient documents.

II. THE INTERNAL TEST

The second test of the reliability of the biblical documents asks, "What claims does the Bible make about itself?" This may appear to be circular reasoning. It sounds like we are using the testimony of the Bible to prove that the Bible is true. But we are really examining the truth claims of the various authors of the Bible and allowing them to speak for themselves. (Remember that the Bible is not one book but many books woven together.) This provides significant evidence that must not be ignored.

A number of biblical authors claim that their accounts are primary, not secondary. That is, the bulk of the Bible was written by people who were eyewitnesses of the events they recorded. John wrote in his Gospel, "And he who has seen has borne witness, and his witness is true; and he knows that he is telling the truth, so that you also may believe" (John 19:35; see 21:24). In his first epistle, John wrote, "What was from the beginning, what we have heard, what we have seen with our eyes, what we beheld and our hands handled concerning the Word of life … what we have seen and heard we proclaim to you also" (1 John 1:1, 3). Peter makes the same point abundantly clear: "For we did not follow cleverly devised tales when we made known to you the power and coming of our Lord Jesus Christ, but we were eyewitnesses of His majesty" (2 Peter 1:16; also see Acts 2:22; 1 Peter 5:1).

The independent eyewitness accounts in the New Testament of the life, death, and resurrection of Christ were written by people who were intimately acquainted with Jesus Christ. Their Gospels and epistles reveal their integrity and complete commitment to the truth, and they maintained their testimony even through persecution and martyrdom. All the evidence inside and outside the New Testament runs contrary to the claim made by criticism that the early church distorted the life and teachings of Christ. Most of the New Testament was written between AD 47 and 70, and all of it was complete before the end of the first century. There simply was not enough time for myths about Christ to be created and propagated. And the multitudes of eyewitnesses who were alive when the New Testament books began to be circulated would have challenged blatant historical fabrications about the life of Christ. The Bible places great stress on accurate historical details, and this is especially obvious in the Gospel of Luke and the book of Acts, Luke's two-part masterpiece (see his prologue in Luke 1:1–4).

III. THE EXTERNAL TEST

Because the scriptures continually refer to historical events, they are verifiable; their accuracy can be checked by external evidence. The chronological details in the prologue to Jeremiah (1:1–3) and in Luke 3:1–2 illustrate this. Ezekiel 1:2 allows us to date Ezekiel's first vision of God to the day (July 31, 592 BC).

Early Roman, Greek, and Jewish sources have well established the historicity of Jesus Christ, and these extrabiblical writings affirm the major details of the New Testament portrait of the Lord. The first-century Jewish historian Flavius Josephus made specific references to John the Baptist, Jesus Christ, and James in his *Antiquities of the Jews*. In this work, Josephus gave us many background details about the Herods, the Sadducees and Pharisees, the high priests like Annas and Caiaphas, and the Roman emperors mentioned in the Gospels and Acts.

We find another early secular reference to Jesus in a letter an imprisoned Syrian named Mara Bar-Serapion wrote a little after AD 73. This letter to his son compares the deaths of Socrates, Pythagoras, and Christ. Other first- and second-century writers who mention Christ include the Roman historians Cornelius Tacitus (Annals) and Suetonius (Life of Claudius, Lives of the Caesars), the Roman governor Pliny the Younger (Epistles), and the Greek satirist Lucian (On the Death of Peregrine). Jesus is also mentioned a number of times in the Jewish Talmud.

The Old and New Testaments make abundant references to nations, kings, battles, cities, mountains, rivers, buildings, treaties, customs, economics, politics, dates, and so forth. Because the historical narratives of the Bible are so specific, many of their details are open to archaeological investigation. While we cannot say that archaeology proves the authority of the Bible, it is fair to say that archaeological evidence has provided external confirmation of hundreds of biblical statements. Higher criticism in the nineteenth century made many damaging claims that would completely overthrow the integrity of the Bible, but the explosion of archaeological knowledge in the twentieth century reversed almost all these claims. Noted archaeologists such as William F. Albright, Nelson Glueck, and G. Ernest Wright developed a great respect for the historical accuracy of the scriptures as a result of their work.

Out of the multitude of archaeological discoveries related to the Bible, consider a few examples to illustrate the remarkable external substantiation of biblical claims. Excavations at Nuzi (1925–41), Mari (discovered in 1933), and Alalakh (1937–39; 1946–49) provide helpful background information that fits well with the Genesis stories of the patriarchal period. The Nuzi tablets and Mari letters illustrate the patriarchal customs in great detail, and the Ras Shamra tablets discovered in ancient Ugarit in Syria shed much light on Hebrew prose and poetry and Canaanite culture. The Ebla tablets discovered recently in northern Syria also affirm the antiquity and accuracy of the book of Genesis.

Some scholars once claimed that the Mosaic law could not have been written by Moses, because writing was largely unknown at that time and because the law code of the Pentateuch was too sophisticated for that period. But the codified Laws of Hammurabi (ca. 1700 BC), the Lipit-Ishtar code (ca. 1860 BC), the Laws of Eshnunna (ca. 1950 BC), and the even earlier Ur-Nammu code have refuted these claims.

ENDNOTES

1   John Lennox, *Against the Flow* (Oxford, UK: Monarch Books Kindle Edition, 2015), Loc 5217

2   Charles Colson, *The Faith* (Zondervan, 2012), p113

3   George Matheson, *Thoughts for Life's Journey* (New York: A.C. Armstrong & Son, 1908), p266

4   Henry Blackaby, *Experiencing God* (B&H Publishing Group, Kindle Edition), Loc 985

5   Dallas Willard, *The Great Omission: Reclaiming Jesus' Essential Teachings on Discipleship* (Harper Collins e-Books, 2006), Loc 970

6   J.R.R. Tolkein, *On Fairy Stories* (HarperCollins, 2014), https://books.google.com/books/about/Tolkien_on_Fairy_stories.html?id=4k8cngEACAAJ&source=kp_cover

ABOUT THE AUTHOR

Jim Phillips has been a follower of Jesus for over fifty years, and he has been a Bible teacher for more than forty years. He is the city director for the C. S. Lewis Institute in Annapolis, Maryland, and his purpose for writing God's Megathemes was to pass on to his children, grandchildren, and readers the truths from scripture that have guided his walk with Jesus and enriched his life. His hope is that these megathemes will increase your love for Jesus and your desire to follow his teachings.